Bible Truth for Marriage and The Home

A practical study on Marriage and the Home
from the King James Bible

Keith Allison

Publisher: Keith Allison

Copyright © 2008 Keith Allison

Cover design by Brenda Nicholson

All scripture quotations are from the King James Bible.

ISBN – 978-0-615-21055-1

Additional copies can be ordered from the Author.
Keith Allison
355 Alfred Taylor Rd.
Demorest, GA 30535

PRINTED IN THE UNITED STATES OF AMERICA

Dedication

I want to dedicate this book to my wife, Carolyn. We were married on February 6, 1976.

Beyond doubt, God in His providence put us together. She is and has been a wonderful helpmeet to me in the ministry. She has been a loving mother to our two daughters, Jennifer and Keisha. Besides being a good wife and mother, she is my best friend.

Truly, we have become one in our marriage relationship. Through these years of our marriage, she has taught me so much by her love and care for our family. And it is because of our own marriage relationship with God's blessings upon it that I have the inspiration to write this book. It is my desire to share these truths so that others can be as happy as we have been.

Acknowledgements

I would like to express my gratitude for the following persons for their devotion and assistance in getting this book ready for the printer. I know they will share with me the joy of knowing that this book will be a blessing and a help to many.

Mrs. Brenda Nicholson for editing and the cover design. Also for her assistance in the overall effort of this project.

Miss Hope Welborn for final proofreading and editing.

Mrs. Sandie Pinkston for proofreading and typing.

A special thanks to our two daughters and their husbands, Jennifer and Austin Harmon and Keisha and David Black, along with our grandchildren for the inspiration and encouragement to write this book.

Contents

Introduction:

"Marriage is honourable in all, and the bed undefiled: but whoremongers and adulterers God will judge" (Hebrews 13:4).

God's estimation of marriage is that it is honorable. Sadly, in our day, so many people no longer view marriage in such a way that reflects the honorable place that God gives it. If we are going to preserve marriage as an honorable institution, then we must go back to the Word of God, and see exactly what God says about marriage. These truths from God's Word must be taught and preached in our churches and should be taught to our children in our homes.

Bookstores are filled with all kinds of books that deal with marriage and the home. Some of these are written from a Christian perspective, while others are written from a humanistic viewpoint.

I have read many good books that deal with the different aspects of marriage and the home. We all as husbands or wives and parents, can greatly benefit from many of these good works. So you may ask, "Why another book?"

Allow me to explain the burden I have for writing this book. First, let me say that I do not consider myself to be a marriage counselor. I have not conducted surveys or collected mass information from husbands and wives about the problems they experience. But this I do know, with all that has been written, and with all the topics and all the classes that are taught, it seems that we are losing the battle for our homes. It is my conviction that we must have God in our homes. We must follow the principles of His Word, allowing the Holy Spirit to enable us in our responsibilities to each other.

We must see marriage and the home in the spiritual state in which God has put it. We must deal with the heart and soul and not just with the head.

As a pastor, as a man of God, it is my conviction that we must submit to the authority of God and His Word to have a Biblical marriage. This book comes from my heart as a husband, a father, and a minister. In this study, I will take the approach of a Bible expositor. We will simply study the Scriptures.

The outline of this book comes from a series of sermons that I have preached over the years. I am sure we will not cover every subject fully and probably not to your complete satisfaction. My intention is not to provide an exhaustive study, but rather a condensed study and hopefully one to the Biblical point.

Bible Truth *for* Marriage

Part One

Chapter 1

The Battle for Marriage

As we consider the battle for marriage, let me say first that this battle is foremost a spiritual battle. In Genesis chapter two, God created Adam and then took a rib from Adam's side and made Eve. It was God who brought the first man and woman together. Then in chapter three of Genesis, the first conflict that Adam and Eve are faced with is a spiritual one. Satan, through the serpent, attacks the very first marriage relationship. His attack on the first marriage was not just to jeopardize the relationship between man and woman, but also to jeopardize their relationship to God.

Satan's goal is to fight against God and everything He is doing. God's plan for humanity involves His plan for the nation Israel, as well as His plan for the Church; we also know that a nation, as well as the Church, is made up of individuals and families. So it stands to reason that if Satan is going to oppose the work of God, then he will oppose the home. He will seek to do what he did with Adam and Eve; he will seek to destroy the relationship between men and women, and then their relationship to God.

As you read the book of Genesis, which gives us the earliest account of man and society, you can begin to see how the Biblical home began to come under attack in various ways. Note the following:

- Polygamy: 4:9
- Adultery: 16:1-3
- Sodomy: 19:4-11

Satan's attack on the home is not just seen in Genesis but all through the Bible. He is constantly chipping away at the very foundation of society which is the home. The following are five areas of marriage that are the target of the enemy.

1. The Pattern for Marriage

In the forefront of the battle for marriage is the Biblical pattern for marriage. We see from the Word of God that marriage is to be between a man and a woman.

"Therefore shall a man leave his father and his mother, and shall cleave unto his wife: and they shall be one flesh" (Genesis 2:24).

In our society today there are a lot of people who are trying to change this. There are several states that have passed civil union laws that make it legal for same sex partners to be united in a union that is to be recognized on equal ground with marriage. The homosexuals are trying to push their lifestyle on America as a normal relationship. They are using our public schools to get at our children, to indoctrinate them on the idea that there is nothing wrong with homosexuality. They are lobbying our politicians to pass bills that would try to silence the Church and its pastors from condemning their lifestyle.

Their sinful lifestyle is portrayed on television as being common and normal, and anyone who disagrees with them is shown to be ignorant and intolerant.

We must not allow the devil and the liberals of our day to win on this all important issue. We must believe the Word of God and take our stand for the principle that marriage is between a man and a woman.

Let's look at just a few Scriptures in the Bible that plainly show that homosexuality is forbidden and is an abomination in God's sight.

"And the LORD said, Because the cry of Sodom and Gomorrah is great, and because their sin is very grievous" (Genesis 18:20).

What was their sin that God said was very "grievous"? In chapter 19 verse 5, we read about the men of the city coming to Lot's house.

"And they called unto Lot, and said unto him, Where are the men which came in to thee this night? bring them out unto us, that we may know them."

They wanted to have a sexual relationship with the men (Angels) that were in Lot's house. Their sin that brought the judgment of God upon them was homosexuality. The name of one of the cities was Sodom, thus we have the term *sodomy*.

In Deuteronomy 23:17 we read,

"There shall be no whore of the daughters of Israel, nor a sodomite of the sons of Israel."

God's will is clear in Leviticus 18:22,

"Thou shalt not lie with mankind, as with womankind: it is abomination."

According to the Word of God these type of sins were part of the reason that God was using the nation of Israel to judge the Canaanites.

"Defile not ye yourselves in any of these things: for in all these the nations are defiled which I cast out before you" (Leviticus 18:24).

It is just as clear in the New Testament as it is in the Old. Writing to the church at Rome, Paul wrote:

"For this cause God gave them up unto vile affections: for even their women did change the natural use into that which is against nature: And likewise also the men, leaving the natural use of the woman, burned in their lust one toward another; men with men working that which is unseemly, and receiving in themselves that recompence of their error which was meet." (Romans 1:26-27).

Paul in his letter to the church at Corinth writes,

"Know ye not that the unrighteous shall not inherit the kingdom of God? Be not deceived: neither fornicators, nor

idolaters, nor adulterers, nor effeminate, nor abusers of themselves with mankind" (I Corinthians 6:19).

The words effeminate and abusers of themselves are words that are describing the homosexual lifestyle.

From verse 11 of this same chapter it is clear that a homosexual can be saved, but it is also clear that if he or she gets saved, then he or she will no longer practice homosexuality. A "homosexual Christian" is a contradiction of terms.

It sickens me to read and to hear about homosexual preachers and churches that accept homosexual members. May God help us in these apostate days to stay true to His Word and to continue to hold to the Biblical pattern for marriage. Marriage is to be between a man and a woman.

2. The Purpose for Marriage

In a later section of this book, we will be looking at what the Bible teaches concerning the purpose of marriage. So for now, I will just briefly mention this threefold purpose for marriage to show that this is an area that is under attack by Satan and those who would destroy the very foundations of a Biblical marriage.

- First we can see that marriage is for **relationship**. *"And the LORD God said, It is not good that the man should be alone; I will make him an help meet for him"* (Genesis 2:18).
- Secondly, we can see that marriage is for **responsibility**. Eve was to be a helpmeet to Adam. In Genesis 1:28, man was charged with the responsibility of subduing the earth and having dominion over all its creatures.
- Thirdly, marriage is for the purpose of **replenishing** the earth. Looking again at Genesis 1:28, we read that man was instructed to *"Be fruitful and multiply, and replenish the earth."*

As we will study later, this threefold purpose of marriage is by God's design and can only be fulfilled in the husband and wife relationship.

This is why there is an attack on the Biblical marriage. Satan is doing everything possible to hinder the purposes of God for mankind. It is easy to see that this modern day attack on marriage is part of the spiritual battle that is being waged against the kingdom of God.

3. The Purity of Marriage

In most wedding vows you will hear this statement or one similar to it: "And forsaking all others, keep thee only unto him (or her), so long as ye both shall live." This means that the couple who is exchanging wedding vows is vowing to separate from and to keep themselves from any other person and to commit themselves totally to their marriage partner.

This is such an important issue that God dealt with it in the Ten Commandments, *"Thou shalt not commit adultery"* (Exodus 20:14). Jesus expands this to include lust.

"Ye have heard that it was said by them of old time, Thou shalt not commit adultery: But I say unto you, That whosoever looketh on a woman to lust after her hath committed adultery with her already in his heart" (Matthew 5:27-28).

From these Scriptures and many others that we could use, we know that God is requiring that a man and woman keep themselves pure both physically and mentally.

We all would agree that this area of marriage is certainly under attack today. Infidelity is common in many marriages. The entertainment industry seems to promote the lifestyle where cheating on one's spouse is normal and is to be expected. Pornography is now rampant and is brought right into the home by the Internet. Much of the music that people listen to is filled with words that suggest an immoral lifestyle.

Truly, the devil is destroying a lot of homes through sins that are associated with lust, passion, and sex. This has always been one of his main methods of ruining marriages.

As believers we should always be on guard concerning this area. We should be cautious about what we watch on television, what kind of music we listen to, and what we read. If you have the Internet, you should also have blocking software and other programs to prevent pornographic sites from popping up.

I know this may not be a popular idea, but you should never allow your children to have a television in their rooms. If you have a television, it should be in a room where, as parents, you know and can control what your children watch. I also think the same thing about the computer if you have the Internet. It should be in a place where any and all members of the family can see what is being viewed.

Remember, a husband and wife can only achieve oneness when both of them have given themselves completely to one another and to no one else. This includes mentally as well as physically. This "oneness" is what Satan wants to keep from happening. This is why purity in the marriage is on the front lines of the battle.

4. The Permanence of Marriage

According to popular statistics, half of all marriages will end in divorce. It is evident from this fact that the devil is successful in his attack against the permanence of marriage. What is so alarming is that there is no difference in the divorce rate between couples who are in church and those who do not attend church.

People do not take vows seriously anymore. In the marriage ceremony a couple will vow, "Till death do us part," but in reality it doesn't take much for them to "part."

Divorce has never been, nor is it today, a part of God's will. In Genesis 2:24, God establishes the principle of the permanence of marriage,

"Therefore shall a man leave his father and his mother, and shall cleave unto his wife: and they shall be one flesh."

The word *cleave* means "to glue or stick together." Man and woman are to come together and become as one. God did not intend for this oneness to be divided or to come unglued.

When Jesus was asked about the reasons for divorce He said,

"Wherefore they are no more twain, but one flesh. What therefore God hath joined together, let not man put asunder" (Matthew 19:6) and in verse 8 he said,

"Moses because of the hardness of your hearts suffered you to put away your wives: but from the beginning it was not so." Jesus Himself was reinforcing the principle of the permanence of marriage.

Divorce happens, and it seems that no family is exempt, but it still is not God's will!

So many children are being raised in a single parent home or in a home where they have a stepfather or a stepmother. Divorce affects so many people, and many never get over it. Couples should carefully consider all the results of divorce and try to save their marriages if possible.

The devil knows that if he can break up a marriage, then he has caused great pain and heartache to everyone involved. And it doesn't stop there. Studies show that children who come from a broken home have a greater risk of divorce than those whose parents stayed together.

Divorce also has an effect on the Church. I believe the Bible teaches that a man who is divorced and remarried is disqualified from serving the church as a pastor or as a deacon. And if a teacher of the church is divorced and remarried, then it takes the punch out of his teaching when he teaches on Scriptures that deal with marriage and the home.

Please do not misunderstand me on this subject. If you have been divorced and have remarried, it may limit your service in church leadership, but you must go on in your relationship to God and the Church. So find your place and serve God and the church in the way in which God will use you and bless you!

5. The Picture of Marriage

Paul writing to the church at Ephesus said,

"Wives, submit yourselves unto your own husbands, as unto the Lord. For the husband is the head of the wife, even as Christ is the head of the church: and he is the saviour of the body. Therefore as the church is subject unto Christ, so let the wives be to their own husbands in every thing. Husbands, love your wives, even as Christ also loved the church, and gave himself for it" (Ephesians 5:22-25).

Paul is stating truth that applies both to the husband and the wife and also to Christ and His Church. He uses the marriage relationship, with the husband and wife and each of their responsibilities, to demonstrate the responsibilities between Christ and the Church. He even states that this is his purpose in writing,

"This is a great mystery: but I speak concerning Christ and the church" (Ephesians 5:32).

This is one aspect of marriage that most writers speak little about. The fact is that the husband and wife relationship is a living, working picture of Christ and the Church. Our position in the Church, the body of Christ, is not just to be preached about but also to be pictured in our lives. This is Christianity modeled, something that is lacking in our day.

When you consider this truth, it becomes more evident why Satan is so aggressive in his attack on the home. Remember, the battle for marriage is a spiritual battle. It goes far beyond just the breakup of a marriage. It is an attack against the very purposes of God concerning His Church.

Chapter II

Before Marriage

Before we look any deeper into the marriage union, I would like to mention some things that I think every single person should consider before getting married. Much could be said on this subject, but I will discuss what I think are the more basic subjects that singles should find out about themselves and their possible future mates.

1. The Possibility of a Single Life

This may surprise you, but marriage is not for everyone. We know that marriage is God's plan and that it is a relationship that is desired and entered into by most people, yet we know people who have lived their lives perfectly content with being single.

It is a shame that our society places so much pressure on people to get married. If people are not married by their late twenties or early thirties, others wonder what is wrong with them. They make jokes about being an "old maid" or make statements such as "Can't you find anyone that will have you?" I hope that we as Christians would be more sensitive to people's feelings and not judge people based on whether they are married or single.

According to the Scriptures, neither the married nor single status is superior. There were many great people in the Bible who were not married. The Apostle Paul in I Corinthians 7:8 said,

"I say therefore to the unmarried and widows, it is good for them if they abide even as I."

Paul was single, and he saw it as an advantage in his service for God, yet he also knew that celibacy was not for everyone. In verse 9 he said,

"But if they cannot contain, let them marry: for it is better to marry than to burn."

He saw his ability to be content as a single man as a gift of God. In verse 7 he said

"For I would that all men were even as I myself. But every man hath his proper gift of God, one after this manner, and another after that."

Many people have remained single to better serve God based on I Corinthians 7:32-33:

"But I would have you without carefulness. He that is unmarried careth for the things that belong to the Lord, how he may please the Lord: But he that is married careth for the things that are of the world, how he may please his wife."

This is not to say that married people cannot wholly serve the Lord, but it seems that God enables some people to stay single for a certain purpose He has for them.

When Jesus was asked about divorce in Matthew 19, He gave such a narrow answer that His disciples said to Him in verse 10,

"If the case of the man be so with his wife, it is not good to marry."

Since divorce was not God's plan and was a serious matter, the disciples thought it best not to marry at all, but Jesus responded in verse 11,

"But he said unto them, All men cannot receive this saying, save they to whom it is given."

Jesus acknowledges that not all people have the ability to be content in a single state.

In general people have a natural God-given desire for the companionship of the opposite sex. In Genesis 2:18 the Scriptures declare God's evaluation of the man He created,

"And the LORD God said, It is not good that the man should be alone; I will make him an help meet for him."

Most people will find themselves needing a companion and will not even consider staying single.

The most common complaints among singles are loneliness, the absence of physical intimacy, and the absence of parenthood. For some this desire is not as strong as it is for others, and they may find themselves happy in a single state and never marry.

The tragedy of our day is that many choose not to marry but still engage in sexual relationships. They want the privileges that go with marriage without the responsibilities of it. Sex outside of marriage is condemned in the Scriptures. It was wrong then, and it is wrong today.

There are many singles who would like to get married, but because of a lack of social skills, they have had a hard time meeting the right person. Some may remain single because of a bad experience in another relationship, such as with an abusive parent or even with a previous sweetheart.

There are those who have put their whole lives into careers and just will not take time to develop relationships.

A person can be happy as a single, and every single should search his or her heart and seek the will of God as to whether he or she can live and be content never to marry. The single life would be better than a bad marriage. The key is to seek and follow God's plan for your life.

2. The Preparation for a Married Life

A. Your Concept of Marriage

As people think about marriage and plan for the day when they will enter into that Holy union, they usually have some preconceived ideas about marriage. The most common concept of marriage is what I call **The Modeled Example of**

Marriage. We get a lot of help in developing our ideas about being husband and wife from our own parents. We may never have thought much about it, but what we saw modeled before us left an imprint with us, whether good or bad.

In my years of ministry I have seen young people marry and have watched as they follow the example that their parents set. There is so much perversion of the marriage relationships today that it is easy for young people to see the wrong examples.

Then there is the **Expected Marriage** that so many couples believe they will have. This is when, during courtship, their emotions are high and each is at their best. They have never seen each other under trials and burdens. Their relationship has not yet been tested with conflict, and they enter marriage with sort of a "fairy tale" expectation. Of course we all know that doesn't last very long.

But then there is the concept of a **Biblical Marriage**. It is our responsibility as parents and as a Church to properly train and teach the principles of marriage based on the Word of God. If couples enter marriage with a Biblical concept, they will begin in the right way and will avoid a lot of conflict later on.

B. Your Compatibility for Marriage

Let's look now at your compatibility for marriage. The word *compatible* means "capable of existing together in harmony."

Before marriage every couple should know without a doubt that they are compatible for marriage. It is a fact that people marry and remain married, but that does not mean they live together in harmony.

Let's examine three basic areas where couples need to be compatible.

First they should be **Compatible in the Faith**. In II Corinthians 6:14, we read,

"Be ye not unequally yoked together with unbelievers: for what fellowship hath righteousness with unrighteousness? and what communion hath light with darkness?"

Paul uses the example of the yoke – a pair of animals were put in the same yoke for the purpose of working, plowing, or pulling a cart or wagon. It was wise to use two steers, or other animals, that were about the same size and the same age. Not much work could be done by yoking up a steer and a horse together. The horse would be too tall and too fast to put in the same yoke as a steer. So the principle of an "equal yoke" can be applied to various areas of our lives.

Simply put, we should be compatible. There should be a similarity or a likeness between the two. A husband and wife should be compatible in their faith. Both should be saved and living the Christian life.

A single person should not even consider courtship with someone who is not a Christian. If one is saved and the other unsaved, there will be a great difference in their views on life.

The unequal yoke doesn't just apply to marriage but to all areas of our lives as well. In the business world, it would be unwise for a Christian to partner with a non-Christian.

Let's read again II Corinthians 6:14 in context with Paul's explanation of the unequal yoke found in verses 15-16.

"Be ye not unequally yoked together with unbelievers: for what fellowship hath righteousness with unrighteousness? and what communion hath light with darkness? And what concord hath Christ with Belial? or what part hath he that believeth with an infidel? And what agreement hath the temple of God with idols? for ye are the temple of the living God; as God hath said, I will dwell in them, and walk in them; and I will be their God, and they shall be my people."

There are three words in this passage that help us to understand these truths. The word *fellowship* in verse 14 means "to co-participate." The word *concord* in verse 15 means "A sounding together, thus harmony."

The word *agreement* in verse 16 is the same as *concord* in verse 15, "a sounding together." The meaning of these words gives us the principle of compatibility.

Every couple considering marriage should examine their compatibility in the faith very carefully. In the area of faith, the questions that should be asked are:

- Are you both saved?
- Are you compatible in doctrine?
- What church will you attend?
- Do you share the same convictions about moral issues?

In courtship it may be easy to overlook and sometimes not consider issues that could affect the relationship after marriage. For example, if a man who is a Baptist marries a woman who is a Seventh Day Adventist, then which church will they attend? Which one will compromise their beliefs? Will they go to church on Saturday or Sunday? And what about the other doctrinal differences they may have?

And it becomes more complicated when children are involved. Will the husband who is Baptist want his children to be brought up in a Seventh Day Adventist Church? Or will the wife who is a Seventh Day Adventist want her children brought up in a Baptist Church? And who will give the answers when the children ask which church is right?

It is easy to see the complications that an unequal yoke in marriage could have. This is why we should honor the principle of being equally yoked together.

It is a real blessing when a husband and wife are united in their beliefs and convictions. This will make it much easier in bringing up their children.

A couple should also be **Compatible in their Family Views.** There should be an understanding of each other's role in the home. Each should understand what the Bible has to say about their responsibility as a husband or wife. Each should know what the other will expect of them in the marriage. Views on child rearing should be discussed before marriage. Will your children go to public school, Christian school, or home school? What about how your children will dress? What about social activities? Do you both agree on how your children will be disciplined?

It's easy to say, "We will decide all that when the times comes," but you may find out that you don't agree on issues that really matter and that can drive a wedge between you!

I know a man who has left his wife and family, and it all started over their son's haircut. The man insisted on short hair, but his wife was willing for their son to have longer hair, and the devil used this to ruin that home.

Another area in family views is your hobbies, whether it is golf, fishing, hunting, sports or, for the ladies, shopping, shopping, and then more shopping. Many a wife sits home alone because her husband is out doing "his thing." There are many husbands who would like for their wives to spend a little time with them instead of with shopping companions.

Many people marry thinking they will change their mates' habits and hobbies once they are married. Let's face it, what we liked to do before we married most of us still do it after we marry.

Thirdly I think a couple should be **Compatible Financially**. Every couple talking about getting married should discuss and know up front what the other person's intent is for their careers.

Where will their priorities lie? Will the husband have to travel a lot, will he work weekends, and is he a workaholic? Does the wife plan on working outside the home? Does she plan on continuing in her job after children come? Is she career driven? This is one area in which marriages are being destroyed every day. Family should always come before a job or a career. Know this before marriage.

What about personal finances? You must find out if the other person is stingy or a free spender. I've seen married couples where one was stingy and the other a free spender, and many times this is a good balance because one keeps the other in balance. But it is important to discuss this, to know each other, to know what to expect, and to know where you might have to compromise with your spouse in the area of finances.

When two people are courting or getting to know each other, I think it is wise to consider personal background concerning the social level of one's upbringing. Please don't misunderstand me on this issue. I may be a little too cautious here, but I do believe that for some couples this could cause problems later. If one was raised in a very wealthy environment, then he or she has grown accustomed to a certain level of living and may know a social status that the other person may have never experienced. Finding contentment in life may be on two different levels for them.

I am not saying they could not be happy, but they could have far different expectations about the size of the house they will buy or in what neighborhood they will live. What about the family automobile? Will it be an averaged priced car or will it have to be the top of the line of the most expensive ones? Again before marriage, find these things out and avoid surprises. You will have enough of them anyway.

C. Your Confidence in God's Will for Marriage

Before marriage you should consider your confidence in the Will of God for marriage. We are told in Ephesians 5:17,

"Wherefore be ye not unwise, but understanding what the will of the Lord is."

I believe we should apply this basic Biblical principle in everything, marriage included. Outside of our getting saved, marriage is the most important decision we will ever make.

God has a perfect will for each of our lives, and He desires to let us know what it is. Through much prayer and counsel from the Word of God, you should have the Peace of God in your heart about the person you are going to marry.

Too often we make our plans and *then* ask God to bless them. What we should do is to find His plans and to walk in them, and then we will have His blessings.

Even though my wife Carolyn and I were young, we both believed that getting married would enable us to better serve God as a Christian couple. We did then, and we do now, believe that it was God's perfect will for us to marry. Having the assurance in your heart of it being God's will can give you strength in difficult times.

God has a plan as to **whom** you are to marry, **when** you are to marry, or **if** you are to marry.

May our prayer be as Jesus' prayer, *"Not my will, but thy will be done."*

D. Communication Before and After Marriage

Communication is essential before and after you get married. It is a fact that so many people are willing to marry someone without discussing the areas of life and marriage that they will face together. Understanding each other will be a life-long project, so you should start before you say "I will."

For men, it is a little harder to talk about issues or about how they think or feel. Sadly, men like to hold things in, while women like to talk things out. As hard as it is, men need to let their future wives know what's going on inside of their heads. Finding out about each other after you are married can put a real strain on your marriage.

Communicating means talking about what you like or dislike. It means sharing with each other your expectations and goals in life. Being able to talk about your problems will bring you closer together. I believe that communication is one of the keys to success in a good marriage, and it certainly is necessary when children come into the home.

As a pastor, I have seen the problems that can arise within a church when its members did not communicate well with each other. I have also seen the blessings that a church can experience because people were willing to talk about and talk through their differences. It never helps to stick our heads in the sand and pretend there is no problem.

Before you and your future spouse get married, begin the process of good communication. On the positive side of this, let me say especially to men, learn to express your love and appreciation to your spouse. Give compliments when they are due. It is a shame that most married couples fail in this area. It is important to maintain the consideration for each other in your speech regardless of how long you have been married.

Before leaving the subject of things to consider before marriage, let me say a word about the relationships with the parents of the couple who plan on getting married. I believe it is the right thing to do for the man to ask permission from and to get the blessing of the woman's parents. A young lady is under the authority of her father until she marries. In the wedding, this authority is transferred to her husband.

There are a lot of newlyweds who have in-law problems in spite of all they do, but by consulting with both sets of parents and seeking their blessing, you can attempt to get started right.

There are occasions when couples seek to get married, but the parents don't like the idea. I know there are cases where the parents' objections are justified, and they may see things about a person that the future spouse doesn't see. But there are also cases when a set of parents would never be happy with anyone their son or daughter wanted to marry. In this situation the couple should try their best patiently to work the differences out with the objecting parents. Also the couple should take a second look at each other because God may be using the parents' objection to the marriage as a way of showing them it is not His will for them to marry.

Chapter III

Building a Strong Marriage: From the Beginning

Carolyn and I were married on February 6, 1976. We started our marriage relationship on that day. That was the beginning of what we have been building on since then. We were as much married then as we are now, but our relationship has developed and matured over these years. Marriage has to be worked on, developed, and experienced. For this reason I refer to this section of the book as Building A Strong Marriage.

We see people who are involved in sports who exercise and train themselves, pushing themselves to the limit, in order to be good at what they do. Business men and women will work tirelessly, sacrificing family and time to make it to the top in the business world. Millions of dollars are spent each year on education, preparing people for jobs and careers. But when it comes to the marriage relationship, it seem like people think that it will just automatically work, without any preparation before or any building process after the wedding. If people in sports or business professionals or just the general public used the mindset that they have about marriage in that it will "just happen" or "it will all work out," then they would fail terribly in what they are doing. To make marriage strong and lasting it must be worked on. Let's see what God says about marriage in His Word.

First we will look at Marriage from **the Beginning**.

We read in Matthew 19:4,

"And he answered and said unto them, Have ye not read, that he which made them at the beginning made them male and female."

Then in verse 8, we read,

"He saith unto them, Moses because of the hardness of your hearts suffered you to put away your wives: but from the beginning it was not so."

When our Lord was asked about divorce, He answered by going back to the beginning, so if we want to understand the Biblical marriage in order to build on God's Word, then we must go back to the beginning.

1. The Purpose for Marriage

I am sure that some would disagree with the simplicity in which I am approaching the Purpose of Marriage. However, without being technical, I believe we should look at what the Bible says and take God's Word on it, even if it is simplistic. Let's consider three Purposes for Marriage.

A. For Relationship

Man was created on the sixth day. In Genesis chapter 1, after acts of creation God said seven times *"it is good."* But after Adam was created and placed in the Garden of Eden, the Bible says

*"And the Lord God said, It is **not good** that the man should be alone; I will make him an help meet for him. And out of the ground the Lord God formed every beast of the field, and every fowl of the air; and brought them unto Adam to see what he would call them: and whatsoever Adam called every living creature, that was the name thereof. And Adam gave names to all cattle, and to the fowl of the air, and to every beast of the field; but for*

Adam there was not found an help meet for him" (Genesis 2:18-20).

Seven times God said, *"it is good,"* but now for the first time He said, *"it is not good."* Loneliness is a terrible thing. Even though he lived in a perfect environment with all the blessings of God around him, Adam still lacked companionship. Remember, it was God, not Adam, who said *"it is not good."*

God created Adam the way He wanted him. In Adam's nature even before "the fall," there was a longing for relationship that all the animals and fowls that God had created could not satisfy. The desire for companionship is simply programmed in the human race. Of course after sin entered the human race, this desire has been satisfied by many means that God never intended. That is why we must go back to the beginning to see God's original plan for mankind concerning marriage.

In order to meet the Divine implanted desire for companionship, God put Adam to sleep, took a rib, and made the woman, Eve. In Genesis 2:23-25 we read:

"And Adam said, This is now bone of my bones, and flesh of my flesh: she shall be called Woman, because she was taken out of Man. Therefore shall a man leave his father and his mother, and shall cleave unto his wife: and they shall be one flesh. And they were both naked, the man and his wife, and were not ashamed."

God, the originator of marriage, performed the first wedding ceremony. Adam now had someone like him, compatible to him, someone to love, and someone to love him. These are the issues of life that really matter. This is where building a strong marriage must begin. It must begin with an understanding that your spouse is a gift from God to meet a divinely created need in your life. You as an individual will grow and develop in your personal relationship with the Lord as you fulfill your role in the marriage relationship - loving your spouse, and being loved. So many people think that things, money, and pleasure are all they need to make them happy, but God tells us that we need companionship to solve the problems of loneliness, and that marriage is God's plan for meeting this need.

B. For Responsibility

The second purpose for marriage that is given in Genesis is   for responsibility. When God created Adam, He had a purpose for him.

"And the Lord God took the man, and put him into the garden of Eden to dress it and to keep it" (Genesis 2:15).

Before the fall, even in the Garden of Eden, Adam had responsibilities with which God had charged him. Man was created with work as a part of his life. Idleness has never been a part of God's plan for mankind. It is true that after sin entered the world, resulting in the curse, man's work would be hindered and made more difficult as we read in Genesis 3:17-19.

> *"And unto Adam he said, Because thou hast hearkened unto the voice of thy wife, and hast eaten of the tree, of which I commanded thee, saying, Thou shalt not eat of it: cursed is the ground for thy sake; in sorrow shalt thou eat of it all the days of thy life; Thorns also and thistles shall it bring forth to thee; and thou shalt eat the herb of the field; In the sweat of thy face shalt thou eat bread, till thou return unto the ground; for out of it wast thou taken: for dust thou art, and unto dust shalt thou return."*

Part of Adam's loneliness was that he did not have a "help meet" for him in his responsibilities. The words *help meet* mean "one suitable for him." When God made Eve, He was making someone like Adam with whom He could share his responsibilities of life. This is a blessing from God that we can still enjoy today. Having a companion by your side as you live your life with all the work that must be done is truly part of the purpose of marriage.

As a pastor I am grateful for my wife, Carolyn, and the help she has been to me in the ministry. She has always been very supportive of me, even in times when she probably did not fully understand my burdens. I could not have pastored all these years as I have without her. I know at the Judgment Seat of Christ it will be revealed as to how much of my ministry and the results we have seen are a result of her faithfulness in being my helpmeet.

In our society it is common for both the husband and the wife to work outside the home. It is easy for a husband and wife to see themselves going their own way, doing their own thing. This is an attitude that can be harmful to a marriage. A husband or a wife should always see himself or herself as a help meet to his or her spouse, regardless of separate jobs, hobbies, etc.

Many people live to work instead of working to live. Our lives is more than our jobs or houses or cars. We must have these things as we live, but they should not be our goals to live. We need to see ourselves as God intended for us to be. We should live to serve God, enjoy life to its fullest, and appreciate the helpmeet that God has given us as we share the responsibilities of this great opportunity of life.

We all need to ask ourselves the question, "Am I truly helping my mate to be and to become all that God wants him or her to be?" From the beginning this has been God's will for the purpose of marriage.

C. For Replenishing the Earth

In Genesis 1:28 we find God's will for mankind from the beginning.

"And God blessed them, and God said unto them, Be fruitful, and multiply, and replenish the earth, and subdue it: and have dominion over the fish of the sea, and over the fowl of the air, and over every living thing that moveth upon the earth."

The word *replenish* means "to fill." God was telling Adam and Eve to fill the earth with children. God in His creation set the principles of reproduction in motion. In Genesis chapter 1 we find the phrase *"after his kind,"* used in verses 11-12 in reference to plant life. In verses 21-25 it is used in reference to fish, fowl, and animals. In verse 22 we find,

"And God blessed them, saying, Be fruitful, and multiply, and fill the waters in the seas, and let fowl multiply in the earth."

It is evident that God was talking about reproduction in this verse, so it is also evident that He is talking about human reproduction in verse 26.

Let's consider the phrase *"after his kind"* in light of the replenishing of the earth. This is in direct opposition to the Theory of Evolution. *"After his kind"* establishes boundaries between the different species of creation. Evolution says that we all came from the same life source over millions of years. I wonder how they will explain away the fact concerning the study of DNA. True science will always agree with Scripture. I believe the more they research DNA, it will be evident that evolution can not be true. As Bible believers we do not need science to confirm our belief, because it is by faith that we simply believe God's Word.

To make it simple, *"after his kind"* means cats produce cats, dogs produce dogs, cattle produce cattle, and humans produce humans.

People are to live by the morals that God has established both in our natures and in His Word. God did not intend for mankind to replenish the earth without any boundaries or guidance. This is where marriage comes in. When God brought Eve to Adam, she was to be his companion, his wife for as long as they lived. She was not to be one among many as it is so often is in the animal kingdom, but the only one. It was not to be a relationship of instinct, but one of love and devotion to each other. Children were to be the product of a loving relationship between a man and a woman within the marriage union.

The devil is doing all he can to destroy the home, to disrupt the family unit, and to remove the boundaries that God has set. One attack against the family is "same sex marriage." It is plain that this type of union cannot produce children. I think it is a great sin against children when our government allows same sex couples to adopt a child. Do not misunderstand me; I am thankful for people who do adopt children, but it should be within the setting of a traditional home comprised of a husband and a wife.

Children are truly a gift from God, but He wants to give them to us through the way that He has ordered and that is between a man and a woman who are in a marriage relationship. May God help us to hold His standard high both in our lives and in our teaching. I believe we will appreciate the marriage relationship that we are in, and the mate that God has given us, when we consider the purpose of marriage from God's Word. Again that purpose is for Relationship, for Responsibility, and for Replenishing.

2. The Basic Principles for Marriage

As we go back to Genesis and look at marriage from the beginning, we see four principles that are necessary for us to build a strong marriage relationship.

"Therefore shall a man leave his father and his mother, and shall cleave unto his wife: and they shall be one flesh. And they were both naked, the man and his wife, and were not ashamed" (Genesis 2:24-25).

These two verses say a lot about marriage and the way that God intended from the beginning.

A. A Breaking

This is seen by the word "leave" in verse 24,

"Therefore shall a man leave his father and his mother."

The principle of breaking is the process of a young man or a young woman leaving home in order to establish their own home. Children still at home are under the authority of their parents, with the father as the head of the home. The Bible teaches us that children are always to honour their parents, but this does not mean that they will always be under their authority. When a man leaves home to get married, he must break away from the life of being in submission to his father and become the head and take a position of authority himself.

The leaving or breaking away of a young man and a young woman in order to get married can sometimes be a very difficult thing to do. It is the responsibility of parents to train and prepare their children for leaving. I know as parents, Carolyn and I wanted to shelter or protect our children as much as possible. It is easy to try to make all the decisions for them in order to protect them. Sometimes the hardest thing to do is to let children grow up and to allow them to make decisions for themselves, but this is all in the process of preparing their breaking away.

I have heard my father talk about breaking mules and horses to work. This is not easy, and it takes time. You are training and teaching these animals to do things they have never done before. Their minds are to be programmed for the type of work for which you are training them. I know children are not animals, but they must be trained. We expect to give them the best education we can to prepare them for jobs and careers. It is more important to help them to be mature spiritually and mentally and to help them be prepared for the day when they leave home.

Sometimes the parents of newlyweds are to blame for some of the problems the couple experiences. Fathers and mothers too often try to run the newlyweds lives for them. We've all heard the jokes about mother-in-laws; sadly, a lot of this is true.

Since the man is to be the head of the home, let's look at three areas of life that this breaking away from his parents will affect.

1. First, there is **independence**. As children grow to maturity, they pass through dependence to interdependence and finally independence. Independence means he must now stand on his own two feet. He is no longer under the responsibility of his parents. He can no longer live under the shadow of his father telling him what to do.

2. Secondly, there is **responsibility**. He now becomes the provider, the protector for his own home. He cannot push his responsibilities off on someone else.

There are so many who want all the privileges of being married without the responsibility that goes with it. This leaving or breaking from one's parents places one in the position of being responsible not only for oneself but for the new home that is being established.

It is sad to see so many husbands who will not take their place in this role of responsibility. Their wives and children suffer because of their selfish choices.

3. Thirdly, we see **leadership**. This leaving takes a man from following his father and puts him in this leadership role. There are so many decisions that a young married couple have to make. These decisions should be made between both spouses, but the responsibility of leadership is placed on the man.

A newlywed couple will often make mistakes in some of their decisions, but it is theirs to make. This does not mean that they should not seek counsel and advice, because they should, but this is the means of becoming one, as they prayerfully try to follow God's plan of having the man as head and leader in the home.

I remember many times in our first years of marriage when Carolyn and I had to make decisions on things in which we had no experience. It would have been nice and easy if our parents could have made those decisions for us, but they could not. It was our life to live, our decisions to make, and we were the ones who lived with the results of our decisions.

All of this is inferred in the phrase, *"Therefore shall a man leave his father and his mother."* Independence, responsibility, and leadership are involved in this breaking from father and mother. Again let me stress how important it is for parents to train and to prepare their children for the day when they will leave to begin their own families.

B. A Binding

"Therefore shall a man leave his father and his mother, and shall cleave unto his wife: and they shall be one flesh" (Genesis 2:24).

The Hebrew word for *cleave* means to "stick to, adhere to." It is a word for glue. The idea is that when a man and a woman marry, they are to be glued together, to stick to each other, or to adhere to each other. When you glue something you are usually attaching two separate items to each other, thus making them one. The two become bound together. This is a binding process. This binding together is exactly what God intended for a man and a woman to experience in marriage from the beginning.

There is a difference between binding and bonding, as we shall see later in the phrase *"and they shall be one flesh."* But for now let's just consider this binding between a husband and a wife. Marriage is a covenant relationship between a man and a woman. In the wedding vows of most ceremonies, the man and the woman will exchange vows of commitment and promises something like this:

"I, John, take thee, Mary, to be my wedded wife, to have and to hold from this day forward, for better, for worse, for richer, for poorer, in sickness and in health, to love and to cherish, till death do us part according to God's holy ordinance; and thereto I pledge thee my loyalty."

Then the woman will pledge her vows likewise. Usually at the end of the ceremony the minister will say "what therefore God hath joined together, let not man put asunder."

Let's look at what Jesus said about the binding or the permanence of marriage.

"And he answered and said unto them, Have ye not read, that he which made them at the beginning made them male and female, And said, For this cause shall a man leave father and mother, and shall cleave to his wife: and they twain shall be one flesh? Wherefore they are no more twain, but one flesh. What therefore God hath

joined together, let not man put asunder. They say unto him, Why did Moses then command to give a writing of divorcement, and to put her away? He saith unto them, Moses because of the hardness of your hearts suffered you to put away your wives: but from the beginning it was not so" (Matthew 19:4-8).

According to popular statistics, half of all marriages will end in divorce. Our legal system has made getting a divorce a simple matter. Our churches have seemed to accept divorce as just a "part of life," but none of this changes the Word of God or God's will. Divorce is not, nor has it ever been, God's will for marriages.

Marriage is meant to be binding, to be permanent, to be lasting even till death. We must keep the pattern for marriage, according to the Word of God, before our people. We must preach and teach what God says about it, even though it may offend some people.

As a pastor who has church members who have been divorced and remarried, I know how touchy the subject is. Nevertheless, for the sake of our young people and for those who may be struggling to keep a marriage together, we must be true to God's Word. The principle of the binding or the permanence of marriage is a foundational truth and is so important to the preservation of Biblical marriage.

C. A Bonding

The third Basic Principle of Marriage from Genesis 2:24 is the principle of bonding. This bonding is seen in the words *"and they shall be one flesh"* and is the unity that a husband and a wife are to experience. The difference between bonding and the binding that we have just looked at is that the binding speaks of man and wife being put together as one. They are bound together for life. The principle of bonding means that *"they **two** shall be **one** flesh"* (Ephesians 5:31). It means that they become a part of each other's lives.

It is possible for a man and a woman to be bound together in marriage, to be husband and wife, yet never really experience the bonding that should take place. It takes only a few minutes to have a wedding ceremony where a couple is bound together, but it takes years for the process of bonding to bring the couple into a state of marital maturity. This is not to say that they are not one flesh from the beginning of their marriage, because they are, but it takes time and experience to fully understand what it means to be one flesh.

The wording *"one flesh"* is found three times in the New Testament. In each of these places they show us something different about the marriage relationship. Let's consider these passages of Scripture.

1. In Matthew 19:5-6 we see in the context that Jesus used this phrase "one flesh," teaching the **Permanence** of marriage.

"And said, For this cause shall a man leave father and mother, and shall cleave to his wife: and they twain shall be one flesh? Wherefore they are no more twain, but one flesh. What therefore God hath joined together, let not man put asunder."

The bonding between a man and a woman is meant to be permanent, until death.

2. The Apostle Paul in his letter to the Corinthians used this phrase in dealing with sexual **Purity**.

"What? know ye not that he which is joined to an harlot is one body? for two, saith he, shall be one flesh" (1 Corinthians 6:16).

The city of Corinth was known for its wicked practices. One of their sins was the prostitution associated with the Temple of Aphrodite. In Paul's warning to the church he said,

"Flee fornication. Every sin that a man doeth is without the body; but he that committeth fornication sinneth against his own body" (1 Corinthians 6:18).

The phrase "one flesh" as used in Genesis 2:24 refers to the sexual union of a married couple. It is God who made man and woman with natural sexual desires, which are to be fulfilled only within the marriage relationship.

Sexual activity outside of marriage, or with someone other than his or her spouse, is condemned in the Scriptures. The word *fornication* is generally used for sexual sins with someone other than one's husband or wife.

The coming together of a married couple in this sexual union is the ultimate in giving yourself to your spouse. It is to be the most intimate form of expressing your love to each other. This is a part of the bonding that takes place between a husband and a wife. It is because of this that God intended sex to be only between a husband and wife.

In the animal kingdom, animals engage in sexual activity through instinct in order to reproduce. It is true that many birds and animals do mate for life, where there is a level of bonding and intimacy, but for many, sexual activity has no intimate meaning. It is not a means of bonding, but simply the fulfilling of a sexual drive. Sadly, this is how sex is treated by many today. There is no intention of bonding or becoming one intimately, but simply the fulfilling of one's sexual interest.

God intends for husband and wife to have sexual pleasure, to bring children into their family, and to become one in this means of bonding. I know that it takes a lot more than just a physical union to have a good marriage, but remember this is God's plan.

Because we all have a natural desire for sexual pleasure, let me leave this subject with a warning. We live in a sex-driven society where anything goes. As Christian couples, as well as singles, we have to battle to keep ourselves pure and clean in this area. We must have godly convictions about what we watch, what we read, how we dress, and where we go.

There is so much unfaithfulness among married couples and so much promiscuousness among singles. Yet we must set the standard high and strive to obey the Word of God in order to preserve our marriages and our homes. Paul had this in mind when he wrote 1 Corinthians 7:2,

"Nevertheless, to avoid fornication, let every man have his own wife, and let every woman have her own husband."

When a husband and a wife love each other and are meeting each other's needs at home, God says this is a preventive against sexual sins. May God help us to fully understand all that's in the words *"one flesh,"* and to allow this bonding to take place between ourselves and our spouses.

3. The wording "one flesh" is also used is in Ephesians 5:31,

"For this cause shall a man leave his father and mother, and shall be joined unto his wife, and they two shall be one flesh."

Paul puts it in context as a **Picture** of Christ and His Church.

"This is a great mystery: but I speak concerning Christ and the church" (Ephesians 5:32).

We will be looking at Ephesians chapter 5 in our next study, so I will be brief here.

From many Scriptures, we know that the relationship of Christ and His Church is seen as Christ being the groom and the Church being His bride. As we have already pointed out, the words *"one flesh"* speaks of the bonding between a husband and wife, the two becoming one. So it is in our relationship with Jesus Christ. When a sinner gets saved, he becomes one with our Lord. As Paul says in Ephesians 5:30,

"For we are members of his body, of his flesh, and of his bones."

When God inspired Moses to write Genesis 2:24, regarding the marriage of a man and a woman and then becoming *"one flesh"*, he also had in mind Christ and His Church. The marriage relationship is a picture of Christ and His Church. Every saved, married couple should reflect by their relationship to each other the relationship between Christ and the Church.

As we leave this principle on the bonding of a husband and wife, let me conclude by saying that a married couple should be one physically, one emotionally, and one spiritually. I believe that our relationship with God will help us to become "one" with our spouses.

D. A Blessing

We see from Genesis 2:25,

"And they were both naked, the man and his wife, and were not ashamed."

We know that this described Adam and Eve's relationship between each other before sin enter into their lives. But let me hasten to say that this describes God's intended blessing for a husband and wife to experience. So as we go back to the beginning to study marriage, it is important that we consider this verse.

Let's consider first the statement *"and they were both naked."* This means literally that they did not wear any clothes. It was after they sinned that they began to wear clothing.

Then we see the words, *"and were not ashamed."* The principle of blessing that we see here is one of intimacy. With the absence of sin, there was also an absence of self consciousness. They experienced total freedom with each other. They had nothing to hide from each other. By never sinning, they did not have any guilt or any thing that would cause them to hide or to keep anything from each other.

After they sinned the Bible says,

"And the eyes of them both were opened, and they knew that they were naked; and they sewed fig leaves together, and made themselves aprons" (Genesis 3:7).

For the first time they experienced guilt which was a result of sin. They felt uncomfortable with themselves. They knew that something had changed. Because of this guilt, this sin, this "uncomfortableness," they covered their bodies. Remember at this time there was still no one else around but God.

To some degree, they lost the freedom that they had experienced with each other before they sinned. And because we all have the "Adamic fallen nature," we too do not have total freedom. We all have sinned and continue to sin.

So the question is asked, "How can we experience this blessing of intimacy if it was partially lost in the Fall?" Sadly, many people enter marriage with what we call "baggage." Many people are suffering from guilt over past sins and relationships. Many deal with no self-esteem, with hurts from childhood or with an abusive past. If people don't like themselves, it is almost impossible for them to believe that someone else can love them.

But thank God for salvation. When we understand that God forgives us, cleanses us from our sins, and forgets them, this enables us to see our worth and our value not as just who we are, but who we are in Christ.

The aprons that Adam and Eve made for themselves are typical of what man does in his attempt to deal with his guilt. Fig leaf aprons would soon dry up and fall off, just like all the man-made religions of our day. But in Genesis 3:21 we find,

"Unto Adam also and to his wife did the Lord God make coats of skins, and clothed them."

The clothing that God provided was representative of Christ's sacrifice for us. This clothing was made of animal skins, thus an animal that was innocent had to die, shedding its blood, because of Adam's sin. This clothing of Adam and Eve by God is symbolic of their restored fellowship to Him. Also because man was now a sinner, it was God's plan for him to wear clothes.

Let me say a word here about this clothing before we move on. God's Word teaches that men and women both ought to dress modestly. In our corrupt society, immodesty is a real problem. Sadly it is not just out in the world, but it is also a problem in churches.

In this tolerant generation, church leaders are afraid to demand a dress code in churches, lest they offend someone. It is my conviction as a pastor that we have the responsibility to see that our church assembly is maintained with reverence and modesty. This "come as you are" attitude is a mockery to the Holiness of God.

Now, back to the question "How can married couples enjoy this blessing of intimacy?" It is not by chance that this blessing is the last of these four principles. These four principles of breaking, binding, bonding, and blessing are in a progressive order. A man and a woman leave home to get married; this is **breaking.** In the marriage ceremony, consummated by coming together physically, there is the **binding** together. As the couple live together and develop their relationship, physically, emotionally, and spiritually, this **bonding** takes place. These all combined lead to the **blessing** of intimacy between a husband and wife.

The longer a couple is married, the more intimate they should become. Intimacy is knowing each other. Intimacy is understanding each other. Intimacy is acting toward and responding to each other in certain ways because you know your spouse. Intimacy is having freedom to be yourself around your spouse, knowing you don't have to hide who you are from him or her. Intimacy is accepting each other as individuals yet knowing you are one. It is having a desire to live, not just for yourself but for your spouse, to make him or her happy.

We have life here as we know it for only a short time, and what a blessing it is to share this life with someone you love in the marriage relationship. This blessing of intimacy is two people, husband and wife, becoming best friends, intimate lovers, and partners together in the race of life. Serving God as a team, they help each other in the roles that they have to fulfill. The strengths of one become a help to the other's weakness.

Marriage is meant to be a wonderful experience, but it will only be that to the extent of it being a Biblical marriage.

3. The Plan for Order in Marriage

When we begin to talk about God's plan for order in the marriage relationship, we open up a very controversial subject. Yet if we are trying to understand marriage from the Scriptures, as God has given His plan to us, then it is necessary that we look very closely at this subject.

We are all aware of the feminist movement, which goes to extreme measures to put women on an equal ground with men. Please do not misunderstand me; I am for equal rights. No person should be treated less than others because of

gender, race, or any other differences. This portion of the
book is not intended to inflate the male ego or to cause any
woman to feel degraded in any way.

Christianity has done great things on behalf of women.
In ancient times women were considered property to be
owned, just like a horse or a sheep. Instead of degrading
women, like many people accuse the Bible of doing, it
actually declares the opposite. The message from God is that
women are in a lofty place of honor.

Many women do not like to hear sermons that talk about
the man being the head of the home. There are some men
who like to remind their wives of this as a means of being a
"scriptural bully." This is not what God intends. As we
examine the Scriptures, we will see just how plain the Bible
makes this subject. We will have blessed marriages when we
have Biblical marriages.

A. From Creation

Let's examine the plan for order in marriage first by
looking at Creation.

In Genesis 2:7 we read of the creation of man,

*"And the Lord God formed man of the dust of the ground,
and breathed into his nostrils the breath of life; and man
became a living soul."*

It is very evident that Adam, a man, was the first human
on the earth. He was created from small particles of the earth
called dust. The Hebrew words for *man* and *earth* are very
similar. Although man was made from the dust, his life came
from the breath of God.

Adam was placed in the Garden of Eden, to dress it and
to keep it. Then in Genesis 2:18 we find,

*"And the Lord God said, It is not good that the man
should be alone; I will make him an help meet for him."* We
then read in verses 21-22, *"And the Lord God caused a deep
sleep to fall upon Adam and he slept: and he took one of his
ribs, and closed up the flesh instead thereof; And the rib,*

which the Lord God had taken from man, made he a woman, and brought her unto the man."

From reading these verses we can see that chronologically man was made first. Also these verses teach us that the woman was made from man. The apostle Paul refers to this in writing to the church at Corinth on the subject of public worship in relationship to the headship of man.

"For the man is not of the woman; but the woman of the man. Neither was the man created for the woman; but the woman for the man" (1 Corinthians 11:8-9).

Again let me state plainly what we have found out from God's Word:

1. Man was created first.

2. The woman was made for the man.

We must accept this if we establish the proper order for men and women in the marriage relationship. I believe this is a fundamental and a foundational principle for marriage.

The Bible gives us God's plan for order in the church, in our governments, as well as in our homes. Without order there is confusion. In 1 Corinthians 11:3 we see this principle of order in a nut shell,

"But I would have you know, that the head of every man is Christ; and the head of the woman is the man; and the head of Christ is God."

We will look at this verse in depth later on, but for now, let me say that this verse teaches what we have already seen from creation, which is the fact that the man is to be the head of his wife and children.

B. From the Constitution of Our Natures

Next we can see the plan for order in marriage by the constitution of our natures.

"Likewise, ye husbands, dwell with them according to knowledge, giving honour unto the wife, as unto the weaker vessel, and as being heirs together of the grace of life; that your prayers be not hindered."

This verse tells us that a husband should understand his wife. He should be considerate of her; he should honour her. And he should do this *"as unto the weaker vessel."* Exactly what does this mean? The word *vessel* is used in other Scripture in reference to our bodies. In 2 Corinthians 4:7,

"But we have this treasure in earthen vessels, that the excellency of the power may be of God, and not of us."

This treasure is salvation through the message of Jesus Christ. Paul says that we have it in earthen vessels. Here the word *vessels* is referring to our human frail bodies, typified by earthen or clay jars. In 1 Thessalonians 4:4 we read,

"That every one of you should know how to possess his vessel in sanctification and honour."

In the context of these verses Paul is talking about keeping one's self pure, abstaining from fornication. Again the word *vessel* is referring to one's body. So in 1 Peter 3:7, we are to understand that the word *vessel* is referring to the body. Peter then, would be instructing husbands to give honour unto their wives *"as unto the weaker vessel."* He is saying that the woman is physically weaker than the man.

Please ladies, do not take offense. Instead of putting you down, this verse actually puts you in a place of honor. Let me hasten to say what this verse is **not** saying. It is not talking about one's intelligence. It is not talking about one's spiritual capacity. This verse is not making a difference between the value of a man and a woman. But it is saying that the man is physically stronger than the woman.

This physical difference has everything to do with the roles of life that God has planned for men and for women. In the creation of man, God designed his body, his mind, and his emotions for the responsibilities of life that he would face. This responsibility includes being the head of his wife and family. It is his place to be the primary provider for his family. Remember man has not always lived in a technological and industrial society. God told Adam, not Eve, that

"In the sweat of thy face shalt thou eat bread, till thou return unto the ground; for out of it wast thou taken: for dust thou art, and unto dust shalt thou return" (Genesis 3:19).

Up until about the last fifty years, having a job meant hard physical labor. I know that there are still a lot of jobs that require hard labor, but you will have to admit things have changed.

After World War II, the job market opened up on a large scale for women. Today in most marriages, the wife works outside the home to help pay the bills. But when you consider the jobs that men and women hold, you will have to agree that some occupations are so physically demanding that it is usually men who do that kind of work. For instance, carpentry, masonry, cement, and most anything that deals with construction. These are some types of work that a machine just cannot do.

I have said all this to point out that, in reality, on a practical basis, we all agree that men in general are stronger than women. I am not pointing this out to create "competiveness" between men and women, but to simply say that God created men to be the primary provider for his family, and in so doing, He gave him a body that would be strong and sufficient for the hard work.

I have read that a man's skull is thicker than a women's. (You ladies will say 'amen' to that.) A man's lungs are larger than a woman's, and the man has more blood than a woman. About 40 percent of a man's weight is muscle, while about 25 percent of a woman's weight is muscle.

The woman, who is to bear children and guide the home, has a body that is suited for her role. Did you know that a woman's shoulders have a different pitch than that of a man? A woman can cradle a baby in her arms for hours, and it is a natural position for her shoulders, whereas a man is ready to give it up only after a little while. This different pitch of the shoulders also keeps a woman from throwing a ball over handed like a man.

In general, a woman will be more tender-hearted than a man. She will be more sensitive to people's needs. She will be more patient with children. All of this is by God's design. He has given women bodies that are suited for giving birth to children. He has constituted her mind and emotions for caring for her family.

Man has been given a body suited to his role as a protector. Traditionally and historically, it has been men who were on the front lines fighting the battles of war. I know today that women play a large role in our military. There are a lot of things that they can do that is needed and important, but I guess I come from the old school which believes that the battlefield is no place for a woman. Again the differences physically teach us this.

Leaving this point, let me say again, that in the constitution of our natures, God has given us bodies and minds that we need to fulfill our roles as men and women. And man has been equipped both physically and mentally to be the head to his wife and family.

C. From Christ and His Church

Finally, we see God's plan for order in marriage demonstrated by Christ and His Church.

We will be looking at Ephesians chapter 5 in detail in our next study, so for now we will briefly look at 5:23,

"For the husband is the head of the wife, even as Christ is the head of the church: and he is the saviour of the body."

This verse gives two different relationships: husbands and wives; and Christ and His Church. In both of these relationships, the order of authority is the same. The husband is head of his wife, and Christ is head of His Church, which is His Bride.

I don't think anyone would deny the fact that the Bible teaches that Christ is the head of the Church. We understand that being under His headship as the Church is a place of blessing for us. It is also true in marriage, the husband is the head of the wife, and this order will bring the blessings of God upon us.

The point is that God has established order. From Adam and Eve until now, it has been God's way for husbands and wives. When people decide to reject God's order, they are only hurting themselves. Marriage will work the best when it follows Biblical truth.

In summary, we have seen order in marriage demonstrated in three ways: First from creation, secondly from the constitution of our natures, and thirdly from Christ and His Church.

Chapter IV

Building a Strong Marriage: From Christ and His Church

In our previous study, we looked at building a strong marriage from the beginning. We saw marriage as God intended it to be from Adam and Eve. Now, we will look at marriage as it can be seen from Christ and His Church. We will be studying Ephesians chapter 5.

1. The Context of the Scriptures

In studying the Bible, one of the first rules to follow is that you must understand the context of the verses you are studying.

When you look at Ephesians chapter five, you will find it to be in the second division of the book. Chapters 1–3 deal with **doctrine**, while chapters 4-6 deal with **Practical Christian duty**. It is common to find this type of division in most of Paul's writings. Doctrine usually precedes duty. What we believe will affect how we behave.

There seems to be a "dumbing down" in respect to modern churches and doctrine. Expository preaching is foreign to many pulpits. We live in a generation where people want a "feel-good" sermon – a sermon without any conviction, any standards, or any absolute truth.

When was the last time you heard a sermon or a series of sermons on doctrine? This is a departure from New Testament teaching on building strong churches and strong Christians.

I am convinced that the lack of doctrinal teaching and preaching in our churches is directly associated with the worldly behavior patterns of the average church member.

Again, let me say that Ephesians 4-6 deals with practical Christian behavior. This chapter on Christ and His Church, seen in the marriage relationship, is a part of the practical duties as a Christian.

A Christian is supposed to be a Christian in every aspect of his or her life. This includes the marriage relationship. So, when we look at all that the Bible has to say about how we should live, whether it is talking about loving one another, forgiving one another, being kind to one another, or putting off the "old man" and putting on the "new man," all of this should be applied to marriage as well. In other words, being a real Christian should make your marriage better. Your desire to please God, in obedience to His Word, will cause you to fulfill your role in marriage to the best of your ability.

It is important to every believer to have his or her priorities in order. It should be: God first, then family, then church. When God is first, He will make a difference in the other relationships we have. Too often people's jobs come first, then pleasure, then family, then church and last of all, God. And then we wonder what is happening to our homes.

Jesus was talking about getting our priorities in order, and putting God first, in Matthew 10:37-39:

> *"He that loveth father or mother more than me is not worthy of me: and he that loveth son or daughter more than me is not worthy of me. And he that taketh not his cross, and followeth after me, is not worthy of me. He that findeth his life shall lose it: and he that loseth his life for my sake shall find it."*

The only way to really find our life is to give it to God. I see this as applying to all areas of our life, marriage included.

So, in the context of Ephesians chapters 4-6, in giving us instructions on how to live the Christian life, Paul gives us the responsibilities of a man and a woman in the marriage relationship.

It comes down to this: If you want a better marriage, you must be a better Christian. I know that it takes both partners to have a good marriage, but you as an individual must have a personal relationship to Jesus Christ. In that relationship He expects you to do your best, and this in turn will help your marriage.

Next, let's look in our context and see what immediately precedes and follows these verses on the family.

In chapter 5:18-19 we read,

"And be not drunk with wine, wherein is excess; but be filled with the Spirit; Speaking to yourselves in psalms and hymns and spiritual songs, singing and making melody in your heart to the Lord."

Here we are commanded to be filled with the Spirit.

To be Spirit-filled is to be controlled by the Spirit. Paul uses being drunk to illustrate his point. When a person is drunk, he is under the influence of the power of the drink. His behavior is altered. He will say things he normally would not say, and he will do things he normally would not do. The intoxicating drink has a life-changing effect on him.

Paul is saying that we are not to be changed by drunkenness, but that we are to be changed by the filling of the Spirit. Every believer is indwelt by the Holy Spirit from the moment of his or her conversion. Paul wrote in 1 Corinthians 12:13,

"For by one Spirit are we all baptized into one body, whether we be Jews or Gentiles, whether we be bond or free; and have been all made to drink into one Spirit."

We are never commanded to be baptized by the Spirit, for this happened the instant we were saved. We also are sealed by the Spirit. Ephesians 4:30 says,

"And grieve not the holy Spirit of God, whereby ye are sealed unto the day of redemption."

But we are commanded to be filled, to be controlled, by the Spirit. This filling is **not** us receiving **more** of the Spirit, but it is us giving more of ourselves to His control. It is possible for believers to go through their lives, involved in church, reading their Bibles, and even praying, yet not fully surrendering to the controlling power of the Holy Spirit.

You may ask, "What does this have to do with marriage?" Why does this command immediately precede our verses on marriage?

Let's look briefly at some of the ministries of the Holy Spirit that He performs in a believer's life and make the application to the marriage relationship.

In John 14:26 we read,

"But the Comforter, which is the Holy Ghost, whom the Father will send in my name, he shall teach you all things, and bring all things to your remembrance, whatsoever I have said unto you."

Here we see His **teaching ministry**. We have God the Spirit living in us to teach us things that we need to know about our life and all that it involves.

God is the originator of marriage; it is His idea. He is the one who has set the rules down for us. He is the one who has made us, man and woman. So who would be better qualified to teach us than He would? I know this line of thinking is not found in a lot of books on marriage, but I think we should look at it from all the Spiritual angles. We should pray that God through His Spirit would teach us and give us spiritual and practical understanding about the marriage relationship. He knows our spouses better than we do ourselves, and He can help us to understand them as well.

In Romans 8:14 we read, "For as many as are led by the Spirit of God, they are the sons of God."

Here we see the ministry of His **leadership**. We are not in this life alone. Thank God that we have the Spirit of God to lead us, to direct our paths. This is so important in the life of a husband and wife. When a couple has surrendered to the Lord and is seeking God's leadership, their marriage can be so blessed. This leadership that is available to us is why it is so important to be filled with the Spirit.

As I think back over the past, I thank God that Carolyn and I have tried to seek God's leadership in our lives. Truly we have been blessed by the ministries of the Holy Spirit.

In the area of marital purity, of being faithful to each other, we read of the importance of having the Holy Spirit in Galatians 5:16-17,

"This I say then, Walk in the Spirit, and ye shall not fulfil the lust of the flesh. For the flesh lusteth against the Spirit, and the Spirit against the flesh: and these are contrary the one to the other: so that ye cannot do the things that ye would."

Notice the first two sins that are mentioned as being works of the flesh in verse 19: adultery and fornication.

"Now the works of the flesh are manifest, which are these; Adultery, fornication, uncleanness, lasciviousness."

Sexual sins are mentioned first out of a long list of sins that can come from the sinful nature.

Because we have a sin nature that would misuse God-given desires for sexual pleasure within the marriage relationship, it is a necessity that we walk in the Spirit. This is the *only* sure effective way of keeping yourself pure, both before marriage and after. The ministry of the Spirit in our lives is vital to our relationship with God and to our relationship with our spouse. It should be our desire to improve both of these, and we can by being filled with the Spirit.

As we continue to look at the context of Paul's writings on marriage, we see that these verses follow the command to be Spirit filled as we have just examined, but we also see that they precede Paul's writings about the **Spiritual Warfare** that we are in *(Ephesians 6:10-18)*.

I find this interesting. It tells me two things: (1) We must be Spirit filled to really have a godly relationship with our spouses, and (2) The relationships with our spouses are not exempt from the attack of our enemy in this spiritual warfare. This being the case, we must then understand that we must put on the whole armor of God in order to win the battle.

In reality the marriage relationship becomes part of the battlefield. Satan's strategy may be to use one (husband or wife) to get to the other. This was his plan with Adam and

Eve. He came to Eve and tempted her, but his objective was to cause Adam, the head of the human race, to sin.

Putting on the whole armor is not just for our sake as an individual, but it is important to the home as a whole. Paul said in Ephesians 6:11,

"Put on the whole armour of God, that ye may be able to stand against the wiles of the devil."

There are two words here that we need to examine.

First, the word **stand**. I think everyone would agree that today it is getting harder to find people willing to take a stand. We need husbands, wives, and children all to stand if our homes are going to survive. We need pastors and preachers who will stand for the Word of God and not compromise in these days. Are you prepared to stand as husband and wife? It is a necessity if our marriages are to survive.

We also see the word **wiles** which means the "craftiness of the devil." How often we underestimate the devil. I certainly am not bragging on him, but he does what he does well. He is smart, he is crafty, and he usually has us figured out pretty well.

We can't afford to give him an inch. We must be on our guard every minute. He will attack when you least expect it. So it is easy to understand why Paul put all these important truths together. We must be Spirit filled, and we must put on the whole armor of God if we are to build a strong marriage.

2. The Commands of the Scriptures

We are looking at Building a Strong Marriage from Christ and His Church. We are studying Ephesians 5:22-33.

I would like to point out three commands given to us in these verses. There are two given to the wife and one given to the husband. All three of these have reference to Christ and the Church.

A. Wives Submit

The first command of this is found in verse 22,

"Wives, submit yourselves unto your own husbands, as unto the Lord."

Please ladies, don't put this book down yet. I will get to the men later, but for now, let's see what God says about how you can contribute to building a strong marriage.

But before we look any farther on the wife's submission, let's first define the word. The word *submission* is a military term, meaning "to arrange or rank under." The idea is that of relinquishing one's rights to another person.

Now ladies, I know that on the surface this may not sound too appealing to you. But stay with me as I try to illustrate this truth by some examples.

Since the term was used in a military reference, let's consider the idea. In our Armed Services today, we have a chain of command. A person starts out as a Private. As he moves up in rank, he may become a Sergeant or a Captain. If he makes it to the top, he may become a four-star General. This chain of command does not imply that one person is better than another person. Yet it is a system where organization can be achieved.

Can you imagine a military of about two hundred thousand soldiers with no organization? It would be total chaos. It would be inefficient. Yet in this system of rank and order, the person who submits is benefited as well as those in command. As a group, the job gets done.

This is the same idea within a marriage relationship. It does not mean that the man is more important than the woman, nor does it mean that he is her superior as we might think of the term. It does mean that God is a God of order. If we have no order, then we have chaos and confusion.

On the fact of God being a God of order, listen to Paul's words,

"But I would have you know, that the head of every man is Christ; and the head of the woman is the man; and the head of Christ is God" (1 Corinthians 11:3).

This verse states God's chain of command. Again it is not talking about worth and value. We see that God is the head of Christ. Does this mean that Christ is less than God or less important that God? The answer is no. We know that Christ is equal with God, that He is even God Himself. But we also know that in God's plan, Jesus the Son of God has submitted Himself to the Father. The submission of Christ is the example for all of us.

In our context we read,

"Submitting yourselves one to another in the fear of God" (Ephesians 5:21).

This is not just for wives, but this command is for all believers. In the context of chapters five and six, there are five relationships that require submission:

1. Mutual submission – between believers (5:21)
2. Submission of wives – to their husbands (5:22)
3. Submission of the Church – to Christ (5:24)
4. Submission of children – to parents (6:1)
5. Submission of slaves - to masters (6:5)

Again the meaning behind the word *submit* is "to relinquish one's rights." This is done in order to serve and to please someone else. It is easy then to see why Paul mentions these five relationships. As we submit to God we relinquish our own ways and desires in order to please Him. By submitting we are putting ourselves in His keeping and in His care. We are recognizing His authority over us for our good. We know that this is the only way we will be blessed, using the submission of the Church to Christ as an example. Paul writes,

"Therefore as the church is subject unto Christ, so let the wives be to their own husbands in every thing" (Ephesians 5:24).

Wives need to make this comparison, because God does.

Can you imagine what the Church would be like if it was not submissive to Christ? To see this, all you have to do is look around you. When you see a so-called church or religious group who does not acknowledge the deity of Christ or identify with His death and resurrection or acknowledge His Lordship in their lives, we call these groups a cult. They are going their own way, doing their own thing. They have no eternal life and are teaching heresy.

This is no different from a wife who will not submit to her husband. She is doing her own thing, going her own way, and instead of building a strong marriage, she is contributing to the weakening of marriage.

Today's feminist movement that seeks to "liberate" women, as they like to refer to it, is doing great harm to marriage and to the home. The lesbian movement says, "Who needs men?" There seems to be a drive behind many women to prove that they are better than men and can go to the top of the world without them.

But if we want to preserve the Biblical marriage, we must keep preaching and teaching from the Word of God. God is the founder of the marriage institution, so I believe He knows best.

The apostle Peter wrote on this subject of submission on the wife's part, "Likewise, ye wives, be in subjection to your own husbands; that, if any obey not the word, they also may without the word be won by the conversation of the wives" (1 Peter 3:1).

He then uses Sarah as an illustration as a holy woman.

"For after this manner in the old time the holy women also, who trusted in God, adorned themselves, being in subjection unto their own husbands: Even as Sarah obeyed Abraham, calling him lord: whose daughters ye are, as long as ye do well, and are not afraid with any amazement" (1 Peter 3:5-6).

In verse five there are four things said about the women of old, of whom Sarah is one: (1) They are called holy women; (2) They are said to have trusted in God; (3) They adorned themselves (according to verses 1-4); and (4) They were in subjection to their own husbands.

This, ladies, is a good example to follow, not the women who are leaving Bible truth for their feminist movements.

For the wife to submit to her husband is for her to recognize that God is the one who has arranged the order of headship. She recognizes that she will be in the place of obedience to the Word of God and by being in the will of God she will be blessed by Him.

Remember our context. The command to be Spirit filled precedes, and the command to put on the whole armor follows. So, ladies, if you are not willing to submit to the headship of your husband, then do not expect to be Spirit filled. Instead of being Spirit filled, you will be grieving the Spirit in disobedience. This then will make you an easy target of Satan's attack. Our victory over Satan can only be possible when we are right with God. So, then we see that there is a lot more at stake here than just your relationship to your husband, but also your relationship to God.

Before we leave this subject, let me say again that the devil is using the fallen nature of men and women to launch his attack on marriage. After Adam and Eve sinned, God said concerning the woman,

"Unto the woman he said, I will greatly multiply thy sorrow and thy conception; in sorrow thou shalt bring forth children; and thy desire shall be to thy husband, and he shall rule over thee" (Genesis 3:16).

Please note the phrase *"and thy desire shall be to thy husband."* What does this mean? For some help in understanding this, we will also look at what God said to Cain,

"If thou doest well, shalt thou not be accepted? and if thou doest not well, sin lieth at the door. And unto thee shall be his desire, and thou shalt rule over him" (Genesis 4:7).

The word *desire* is the same in both passages. From the context and the comparison of both of these Scriptures, it is evident that God was saying that the desire of the woman would be to rule over her husband, but he was to rule over her according to God's plan.

To Cain, God was saying that sin sought to rule over him, but he was to master sin in his life. From this we see that because of Eve's sin, there would be a weakness or an area of problem for the woman in submitting to the headship of her husband. Again we go back to what we saw from the beginning: the battle for marriage is a spiritual battle.

A woman who truly seeks to please God and to be a godly wife will recognize that she, from her fallen nature, has a tendency to resist the headship of her husband, and by recognizing that this is real, she then can seek to address this area with prayer and with application of the Word of God.

I am not implying that all women have the same level of problem with this. There are many godly wives who know and understand their roles within marriage and are setting a godly example.

You have heard it said that admitting you have a problem is half the effort in solving the problem. Because of our sin nature, because we live in a fallen world, both men and women have to deal with their own weaknesses.

B. Wives Reverence

The second command given to wives in this context is found in Ephesians 5:33b, *"and the wife see that she reverence her husband."*

The Greek word translated *reverence* is *phobeo*. It means "to fear." This fear is a reverential fear on the part of a wife for a husband. It does not mean that she is to be afraid of him as if he would hurt her or mistreat her. Remember what John wrote,

"There is no fear in love; but perfect love casteth out fear: because fear hath torment. He that feareth is not made perfect in love" (1 John 4:18). A fear like this would create a bad relationship in the marriage.

Sadly, there are a lot of women who live in fear and torment because of an abusive husband. A man who beats a woman is a poor excuse for a man. He is more like a spineless coward. If he wants a fight, why doesn't he fight someone about six inches taller than he is and who out weighs him by fifty pounds? I don't think he would like the odds, so to make himself feel tough, he hits a woman who usually is smaller than he is. We all have heard about the wife who beats her husband. This is rare, but it does happen.

Again, this is not the motive or the type of fear that Paul is talking about. So what is he talking about when he tells the wives to reverence their husbands?

In Proverbs 1:7 we read,

"The fear of the Lord is the beginning of knowledge: but fools despise wisdom and instruction." Again in Proverbs 3:7 we read, *"Be not wise in thine own eyes: fear the Lord, and depart from evil."*

Here are two verses that tell us to fear the Lord. There are many more verses throughout the Bible that teach us the same thing.

Just like Paul explains in Ephesians, this fear is not the fear that causes torment, but it is a healthy fear. It also speaks of reverential fear, a holy awe, a reverence for who God is, recognizing His authority over us and our place of submission to Him.

For a wife to reverence her husband means that she sees him as God's man, whom God hath made the head of the home. She is recognizing a divine order. It is the same way that we are to recognize God's authority over us, whether it is Christ as head of the Church, or our subjection to human government that God has ordained, or His divine authority in the Church as it is seen in the Pastor or the Shepherd over the flock.

The wife will not submit to her husband if she does not reverence him. I believe this reverence will be seen in the respect she shows her husband. Respect is the one thing that a man needs to know that he has from his wife. A woman wants to be loved and made to feel needed by her husband. It is important for her to know that she truly is a vital part of his life.

We often hear all that men need to do is to make their wives happy. Yet there is a lot we must do, as I will discuss later. Here we need to get the message to wives that if you really want to improve your relationship to your husband, then give him the respect he should have.

I know a lot of men may not be the husbands they need to be. They may come short in a lot of ways, and by their actions you may think they do not deserve to be reverenced. But their failures do not give the liberty to fail. You are responsible to God for your obedience to the Word of God.

Your obedience to God is to be your main motive in your submission and reverence to your husband. Look again at what Paul wrote,

*"Wives, submit yourselves unto your own husbands, **as unto the Lord"** (Ephesians 5:22).*

It says *"as unto the Lord."* Always remember that your relationship to God is first, so obey Him above all. Listen to what Peter says,

"Likewise, ye wives, be in subjection to your own husbands; that, if any obey not the word, they also may without the word be won by the conversation of the wives" (1 Peter 3:1).

Peter is saying that an unbelieving husband can be won to God by the wife obeying God in the area of submitting and reverencing her husband. Ladies, if you want to be treated like a queen, then treat your husbands like a king.

As a man myself, it is important for me to know that I have the respect of my wife. I want others to respect me, but I *need* Carolyn's respect. This is not inflating the male ego; it is the way God designed men. I believe every man wants his wife to be proud of him. A man is success oriented. It is important to him to know that he is accomplishing something in life. It is also important to him to have a companion who is sharing his accomplishments with him. Ladies, you very well know that it is hard for your husbands to talk about things like this. He may not even be able to tell you himself in words what he needs, but he does need your respect and reverence.

C. Husbands Love your Wives

We now come to the third command given in Ephesians 5:22-33. Paul writes to the husbands and says,

"Husbands, love your wives, even as Christ also loved the church, and gave himself for it; That he might sanctify and cleanse it with the washing of water by the word, That he might present it to himself a glorious church, not having spot, or wrinkle, or any such thing; but that it

should be holy and without blemish. So ought men to love their wives as their own bodies. He that loveth his wife loveth himself. For no man ever yet hated his own flesh; but nourisheth and cherisheth it, even as the Lord the church" (Ephesians. 5:25-29).

As you read verses 25-29, notice how many times Paul uses the word "as." Six times he uses it in a comparative sense. We have just seen how a wife is to submit to her own husband *as* unto the Lord. Her submission to her husband is to be reflective of her submission to the Lord.

Her submission is also to picture the Church's submission to Christ as the head of the Church,

"Therefore as the church is subject unto Christ, so let the wives be to their own husbands in every thing" (Ephesians. 5:24).

Now we see the word "as" used in reference to the husband's love for his wife.

"Husbands, love your wives, even as Christ also loved the church, and gave himself for it" (Ephesians 5:25).

So now, when we look at the husband's responsibility to love his wife, Paul says it is to be *as* Christ loved the Church.

It is plain then that if we study Christ's love for the Church, then we will understand how a man is to love his wife. We will look at a threefold love that Christ has for His Church and make the application to the husband.

1). With a Gracious Love

By gracious I mean that His love toward us was undeserved. The word "love" that is used in Ephesians 5 is the *Agapo*, or the love that God is.

"He that loveth not knoweth not God; for God is love" (1 John 4:8).

This is a self-sacrificial love, a love that impels the one loving to give himself in self sacrifice for the well being of the one who is loved.

Paul writes about God's gracious love in Romans 5:6-8,

"For when we were yet without strength, in due time Christ died for the ungodly. For scarcely for a righteous man will one die: yet peradventure for a good man some would even dare to die. But God commendeth his love toward us, in that, while we were yet sinners, Christ died for us."

As you read the Scriptures, it is evident that no one deserves the love of God. It is only by God's grace, His unmerited favour towards us, that we are saved.

"For by grace are ye saved through faith; and that not of yourselves: it is the gift of God" (Ephesians 2:8).

Again Paul writes:

"For we ourselves also were sometimes foolish, disobedient, deceived, serving divers lusts and pleasures, living in malice and envy, hateful, and hating one another. But after that the kindness and love of God our Saviour toward man appeared, Not by works of righteousness which we have done, but according to his mercy he saved us, by the washing of regeneration, and renewing of the Holy Ghost" (Titus 3:3-5).

I believe everyone will agree that God set His love upon us while we were sinners. It was God who took the initiative in our salvation. We were dead in sin, and because of this deadness to spiritual things we were not seeking God. Paul writes,

"Because the carnal mind is enmity against God: for it is not subject to the law of God, neither indeed can be. So then they that are in the flesh cannot please God" (Romans 8:7-8).

We could go on with many Scriptures that point out the grace of God toward us. We were sinners, undeserving of His love, yet He set His love upon us.

Let me hasten to say that I am not implying that the wife is undeserving of her husband's love. This is not what Paul is emphasizing in Ephesians 5. Instead of emphasizing the person who is loved, he is emphasizing the one who is loving. In our context he is stressing Christ's love for the

Church and man's love for his wife. But we still must see this as a gracious love in order to understand a husband's love for his wife.

Marriage is a covenant between a man and a woman. Listen to the words of Malachi,

"Yet ye say, Wherefore? Because the Lord hath been witness between thee and the wife of thy youth, against whom thou hast dealt treacherously: ***yet is she thy companion, and the wife of thy covenant"*** (Malachi 2:14).

When you look at marriage as a covenant relationship between a man and his wife, then you can begin to see how a man is to love his wife with a gracious love. The husband is to love his wife as an action of his will. He is to love because of the commitment he has made to her in this covenant. This is not to say that he is not to be emotionally in love with his wife. But we all know that you can not always trust your emotions.

We hear people saying, "I just don't love him (or her) anymore." This is a love based on emotions. In other words, if one's spouse does everything right and acts the way he or she should, then the spouse will love him or her.

This kind of love is selfish in nature, because the one loving has set conditions on which he or she can love his or her spouse. But God's love toward us is unconditional. We fail Him all the time, we disappoint Him with our actions, yet His love toward us does not change. This is a gracious, unconditional love, and this is how a man is to love his wife.

During courtship, a couple sees the best in each other. They are emotionally thrilled with each other. It seems as though they are headed for the first perfect marriage. Love is wonderful, and life is great. Then after the wedding, they began to see their spouse when they are not at their best, when they act a little more human.

A young married couple will find out how each person reacts to hardship, financial problems, and just the stress of sharing life with someone else. And then children come along, with all the changes of life that they bring.

It is easy to see how every couple must face change in their lives. But a love that comes from the will, from the very heart of a person who chooses to love his or her spouse because they have committed themselves to each other for life, this type of love will last. It is a love that can endure all the disappointment in life. Again it is a gracious, unconditional love. This is the love by which a man is to love his wife.

Let me also point out that the husband is to be the one to take the lead in this loving relationship. Wives are taught "to love their husbands."

"That they may teach the young women to be sober, to love their husbands, to love their children" (Titus 2:4).

It seems to me that, just as Christ loves the Church, which means He *first* loved us, the husband is to take the initiative in loving his wife.

When the husband loves as he should, then the wife's love will be a responding love to his. In the same way our love as the Church is a responding love to God's love,

"Herein is love, not that we loved God, but that he loved us, and sent his Son to be the propitiation for our sins" (1 John 4:10).

Again John writes,

"We love him, because he first loved us" (1 John 4:19).

Men may like the fact that the Bible teaches that they are the heads of their wives, that God has put them as the leaders in their homes. But with this headship comes responsibility that many men are not facing up to. Privileges come with responsibility and with accountability.

We have all heard that marriage is a fifty-fifty relationship. It would be more accurate to say it is a sixty-forty relationship, with the greater responsibility being on the husband.

Men want their wives to be in subjection to their headship, and they should, but we men also should want just as much to love our wives with this gracious love that God would have us to.

2) With a Giving Love

Not only are men to love their wives with a gracious love, but also with a giving love.

"Husbands, love your wives, even as Christ also loved the church, and gave himself for it" (Ephesians 5:25).

Some of you men might think that so far I have been a little hard on you, but we have just started. It doesn't get easier but actually harder for us. So let's look at this giving love that we should have for our wives.

Let's go back to something we have already mentioned. In looking at a wife's submission, we pointed out that there is a mutual submission among all believers,

"Submitting yourselves one to another in the fear of God" (Ephesians 5:21).

This means just what it says. When you take this verse and put it in the context of verse 25, *"Husbands, love your wives, even as Christ also loved the church, and gave himself for it,"* then you will understand that a husband, in loving his wife, will submit with this mutual submission in giving himself for her.

Remember, the idea behind submission is relinquishing one's rights to another person. Let's consider Christ's love for the Church, a love that caused Him to give Himself for it.

Let's think about a gift for a few moments. We have many occasions where we will give someone a gift. It may be at Christmas, on a birthday, and if it is for a spouse, on a wedding anniversary. We give gifts to show our love and appreciation to someone else. We also receive gifts as a token of someone else's love toward us. We even use the phrase, "It's not the gift but the thought that counts." But it does mean a lot to us when we know that someone has spent a lot of money, time, or thought to get us a gift in order to show their love for us. This is a love that gives.

Let's look at how God has loved us.

"For God so loved the world, that he gave his only begotten Son, that whosoever believeth in him should not perish, but have everlasting life" (John 3:16).

This verse tells us that God loved us, but it also tells us how He showed His love. He showed His love by giving, not just any gift, but He gave His only Son. This is the greatest gift He could give and, being God, He gave Himself.

The point that I am trying to make is that a husband is to love his wife with such a love that he is willing to give up his own life for her. This is how Christ loved the Church. Listen to Paul speaking to the elders from Ephesus,

"Take heed therefore unto yourselves, and to all the flock, over the which the Holy Ghost hath made you overseers, to feed the church of God, which he hath purchased with his own blood" (Acts 20:28).

Jesus paid the highest price for the Church – His own blood.

Let's examine some practical ways the Church is benefited by this giving love that Christ has for the Church.

1) First we see that **He gives His presence to the Church**. Listen to the words of John the apostle:

"And I turned to see the voice that spake with me. And being turned, I saw seven golden candlesticks; And in the midst of the seven candlesticks one like unto the Son of man, clothed with a garment down to the foot, and girt about the paps with a golden girdle. His head and his hairs were white like wool, as white as snow; and his eyes were as a flame of fire; And his feet like unto fine brass, as if they burned in a furnace; and his voice as the sound of many waters" (Revelations 1:12-15).

John tells us in verse 20 that the seven candlesticks are the seven churches. What I want you to see is that John saw Christ in the midst of these seven churches, or His presence in His Church. You cannot separate the head from the body without killing both. And we know that Christ the head is not going to be separated from His body, the Church.

As saved people, both individually and corporately as the Church, we are the Temple of the Holy Spirit. Having Christ's presence is one of the most encouraging truths we can know. So it is in the marriage relationship. When a husband loves his wife, as Christ loved the Church, then he will give her his presence. Men often try to substitute their presence with presents.

A man may think that if he can give his wife a fine house, a new car, expensive jewelry, and other material things, then she will be happy. All these things are nice, and there is nothing wrong with providing your family with the finest things that money can buy. But remember that Christ gave **Himself.**

Many husbands give themselves to a career. Many have hobbies that demand a lot of time. There are a lot of things and circumstances that we all allow to take so much of our life.

Remember when you were courting your wife or husband? Remember all the time you spent together? You would make the time and sacrifice whatever it took to be with the person you loved. But after you said "I do," what happened? You won the heart of that young lady by giving yourself to her. And this is the very thing that you need to continue to do. You can not make her happy with things. Of course these things are a part of expressing your love to her, but give her yourself.

This giving love is not a selfish love; it is a love that will relinquish one's own will in order to please someone else. Listen to the words of Jesus the night before His suffering and death,

"And he went a little farther, and fell on his face, and prayed, saying, O my Father, if it be possible, let this cup pass from me: nevertheless not as I will, but as thou wilt" (Matthew 26:39).

This is the ultimate example of submission and also the willingness of love to give.

Men, we need to face the facts. We need to spend more quality time with our wives. And I am not talking about just the things you like to do, but share time doing what she likes. Let her know you love her enough to give yourself to her. She needs you to listen to her problems, to try and understand her trials and also to enjoy with her the things that make her happy. It just boils down to the fact of companionship. She needs you and you need her.

(2) **Christ gives His Planning to the Church.** As the head to the Church, Christ provides leadership. Again listen to the words of John,

"And he had in his right hand seven stars: and out of his mouth went a sharp twoedged sword: and his countenance was as the sun shineth in his strength" (Rev. 1:16).

He then goes on to tell us in verse 20 that the seven stars are the angels of the seven churches. In other words, these stars or angels are the messengers to these churches, and Christ has them in His hand. This tells us that He is in charge of His Church, and that He is providing, through His plans, leadership to the Church. So Christ in loving His Church gives of Himself in planning and the execution of those plans.

It is in this sense then that a man should love his wife. He should have a desire to fulfill his responsibility to his wife in providing direction and leadership. I am in no way suggesting that the wife should not be involved in making leadership decisions. Every decision that a couple makes should be discussed and prayed over.

This is part of having good communication in a marriage. No man who truly loves his wife will be so insensitive to her and her opinions that he will disregard her and do what he wants. I know personally that there have been times when Carolyn has provided insight into our decisions, and it has kept me from making a huge mistake. So by all means, please talk out decisions that have to be made that will affect your marriage.

There is a blessing here that we must not overlook. As a believer, it is wonderful to know that our lives are in the hands of the Lord. He has committed Himself to us and to our care. We do not have to find our own way, we can trust in Him. It is in this light that we need to see how the wife can be blessed, knowing that her husband is bearing the burden and the responsibility of providing leadership and direction. We go back to the principle of how God has made us for our different roles in life. God has made man both physically and mentally to carry this responsibility.

Again let me say, lest I am misunderstood by you ladies, that without the management and the skill that most wives provide, their husbands just couldn't handle the household's day to day responsibilities. But let me hasten to say that I have heard many wives complain about their husbands putting this entire burden on them. Men, it is our responsibility. This is the way God has designed it, and we will be benefited by living in obedience to God's Word.

(3) **Christ provides for the Church.** Out of His love for the Church, He provides us with what we need both spiritually and physically.

Paul writes,

"For no man ever yet hated his own flesh; but nourisheth and cherisheth it, even as the Lord the church" (Ephesians 5:29).

From this verse we see how the Lord provides for His Church. The word "nourisheth" carries the idea of nurturing, and it implies "feeding." It can include all that is necessary in caring for someone. In Ephesians 6:4 it is used for bringing up children.

The fact that the Lord nourishes His Church means that He is going to provide everything we need. I believe this is talking about our material and physical needs as well as our spiritual needs. Note again what Paul said, *"for no man ever yet hated his own flesh"* (vs.29). When we think of Christ and the Church being one, which we are, then we can understand how Christ will nurture His own body.

We are given the promise,

"But seek ye first the kingdom of God, and his righteousness; and all these things shall be added unto you" (Matthew 6:33).

What a comfort to know that Christ can and will provide for us. This is not just on a personal level, but He also will provide for the local church as well. His love toward us is a giving love, a love that gives provisions.

So it should be between a husband and a wife. The husband, in loving his wife as Christ loved the Church, will love her with such a giving love that it is a pleasure to be the provider in the home. The responsibility of providing for the family is upon the husband.

I know in our modern society, both the husband and the wife usually work. To be very honest, most couples are not willing to have less in order for the wife to stay home. In a lot of cases, the wife chooses to work; she doesn't want to stay home. Many women have believed the lie of the devil that says a woman has to have her own career, to be financially independent of her husband. Many couples have separate bank accounts, which I do not think is a good idea.

As husband and wife, we do have our individual identities, but in the marriage covenant we become one. And the more you try to separate the two and try to maintain an individual identity, you are just providing the devil with more areas to divide you on.

Please do not misunderstand me. I am not saying that women should not work, but according to the Word of God, a woman's first priority should be her home. Paul writing to Titus said,

"To be discreet, chaste, keepers at home, good, obedient to their own husbands, that the word of God be not blasphemed" (Titus 2:5).

Every wife should examine her heart and should seek to be the wife God expects her to be, to be a "help meet" to her husband. And if there are children, then she first of all has a responsibility to her children.

There are also many men who want their wives to work so that he can afford all his "toys." Let's face it – humans are very selfish. We want what we want and are not willing to sacrifice for the way God intends for us to live.

I've said all of this to say that, according to the Word of God, God puts the responsibility of providing for the family upon the husband. I also believe it is the man's place to lead in the decisions that make it practical for his wife to stay home with the children. Every man should look practically at his income and take the lead in determining what kind of house, cars, and anything else they purchase.

If there are no children, then the wife may have more liberty to work, but the danger is that they become accustomed to both incomes, and then when children do come along, they can't afford for her to stay home.

So men, love your wives with a love that provides. Take your responsibility and lead your home in a direction that will give your wife the freedom from the burdens of providing. Just as every saved person can rest in the provisions of Christ, every wife should not have to bear the worries about providing for the family.

In leaving this subject, let us hear Paul's strong words to Timothy about a man providing for his house.

"But if any provide not for his own, and specially for those of his own house, he hath denied the faith, and is worse than an infidel" (1 Timothy 5:8).

(4) Christ's Love for His Church is **A Protecting Love.** Let's read again Ephesians 5:29,

"For no man ever yet hated his own flesh; but nourisheth and cherisheth it, even as the Lord the church."

We saw how the word "nourisheth" is related to Christ giving *Provisions* to His Church, but now we will see that the word "cherisheth" is related to Him *Protecting* His Church.

The word *cherish* primarily means "to heat, to soften by heat, to keep warm." It is illustrated by birds covering their young with their feathers. We all know how a bird will build a nest, and then lay her eggs. She then will sit on them, providing the needed heat until they hatch. She then will bring food to them until the day they are ready to fly away. She will watch over them with a protecting eye.

This past spring, I was sitting on our front porch. There was a bird that had built her nest in our shrub next to the house. I watched as the bird hopped around the yard and then suddenly, she flew to the base of the shrubbery, where she proceeded to pitch a fit. Then out came a black snake about three feet long. The bird chased the snake across the yard until it disappeared into the woods. The bird was giving protection to its young.

Now that we understand more about the word *cherish*, let's see how Christ protects His Church. Listen to Jesus own words,

"And I say also unto thee, That thou art Peter, and upon this rock I will build my church; and the gates of hell shall not prevail against it" (Matthew 16:18).

In this verse Jesus is assuring us of the stability and the safety of His Church. Knowing that the Head of the Church is the sovereign Son of God certainly gives us the comfort that He can provide protection.

As we study the New Testament, we see His hand in the formation of the Church. We see His hand in the preservation of the Church during times of persecution. We even read about the future of the Church in prophecy. We see the Church triumph in the book of Revelation.

There have been political assaults, economic hardships, and a great slaughter of many men and women, yet today there is the Church of God, strong and vibrant, and there will be a Church for Him to come for at the Rapture.

We cannot keep ourselves, and if it was left up to us and to our power, the Church would have been extinct long ago. But thank God He is the one who is keeping and protecting His Church.

The Church could not stand against the devil and his demons if it were not for the enabling power of the Holy Spirit. We have the Word of God as the "sword of the Spirit." We have the armour of God to put on in order to stand. We have the strength that comes from the fellowship of other believers. All these, and much more, are ways that Christ protects His Church.

So this protecting love of Christ that He gives to the Church is an example and an illustration of how a man is to love his wife, and in doing so, he will do what it takes, even in giving his own life to protect his wife.

When we talk about a man protecting his wife and children we automatically think about protecting them from physical harm. This he should do, but his responsibility of protecting them goes a lot deeper than this. The man being physically stronger than the woman is built to be the protector. But it takes more than just physical strength to fulfill his role. There are moral and spiritual dangers that he must be aware of as well.

This is an area where Adam failed. He should have been more aware of what Eve was getting in to. This is why the fall of man is placed upon Adam's shoulders rather than Eve's. It was Adam's responsibility, being the head of his home, and he failed to protect Eve from Satan's attack.

A lot of men leave it to their wives to be the spiritual leader, but God holds us men responsible for taking the oversight in our families. It is the man's place to steer his wife in the right direction in spiritual matters. He is to take the lead in setting safeguards for his family when it comes to moral issues.

The husband is to be just like the watchman on the wall. He is to be alert, and warn his family about the approach of the enemy.

We need men who are willing to be men, men who understand their God-given responsibilities. If we are going to see marriage endure all the attacks that are coming against it, we are going to have to get back to preaching and practicing God's Word.

3) With a Goal-Seeking Love

We have seen how a man is to love his wife with a Gracious love, a Giving love, and now let's look at a Goal-seeking love. Let's read again in our context:

> *"Husbands, love your wives, even as Christ also loved the church, and gave himself for it; That he might sanctify and cleanse it with the washing of water by the word, That he might present it to himself a glorious church, not having spot, or wrinkle, or any such thing; but that it should be holy and without blemish. So ought men to*

love their wives as their own bodies. He that loveth his wife loveth himself" (Ephesians 5:25-28).

These verses tell us that Jesus gave Himself for the Church, but they also tell us that He had a goal or purpose for the Church. In verse 26 it says, *"that he might sanctify and cleanse it."* This is speaking about the sanctification of the Church.

God did not save us for us to stay where we are, but through His Word and by His Spirit, He seeks to mature His Church and to conform believers into the image of Christ. Then in verse 27 we are told that,

"he might present it to himself a glorious church, not having spot, or wrinkle, or any such thing; but that it should be holy and without blemish."

This is Christ's goal for His Church.

One day the Church will be presented to Christ as His bride. John wrote,

"Let us be glad and rejoice, and give honour to him: for the marriage of the Lamb is come, and his wife hath made herself ready. And to her was granted that she should be arrayed in fine linen, clean and white: for the fine linen is the righteousness of saints. And he saith unto me, Write, Blessed are they which are called unto the marriage supper of the Lamb. And he saith unto me, These are the true sayings of God" (Revelation 19:7-9).

What a wonderful day that will be! Without exception, all the wedding ceremonies that I have performed seem to have put the emphasis on the bride. All eyes are upon her as she walks down the aisle to join her husband-to-be. And in every wedding the bride has done everything possible to make herself beautiful as she is presented to her husband.

This is exactly what Christ's goal is for His Church. He wants her to be exactly what God has foreordained for her. Throughout all eternity, the angels, the Old Testament saints, the tribulation saints, and the millennial saints will behold the Bride of Christ. The Church as the Bride of Christ will forever magnify the wisdom and grace of God. And the

Bride will reflect the glory of her Groom, the Lord Jesus Christ. This is Christ's goal for His Church.

Men are told to love their wives as Christ loved the Church. Christ loves the Church with a love that has a purpose behind it – a love that seeks for the growth and spiritual development of the wife. So men are to love their wives.

This is not to imply that the husband will be more spiritual than his wife. In many cases the reverse is true. As a pastor, I have seen for years that often the wife has a closer walk to God than her husband. Where would our churches be without the contribution of godly women?

But this fact does not mean this is the way it should be. God still puts the responsibility of being the spiritual leader upon the man. He is to have a desire to see his wife become a great woman of God. He is to set the example with his own dedication to the Lord. He is to help set the environment for his wife's spiritual growth.

Paul gives a little insight to this in his writings,

"And if they will learn any thing, let them ask their husbands at home: for it is a shame for women to speak in the church" (1 Corinthians 14:35).

You can see from this verse the influence the husband can have on his wife about spiritual things at home.

Paul writing to Timothy about the qualifications for a bishop says,

"For if a man know not how to rule his own house, how shall he take care of the church of God?" (1 Timothy 3:5).

The word *rule* means "to stand before." This implies that he stands before them as a leader. As he leads his family, he will lead the church.

All of this points to the fact that the husband is to love his wife with a goal of seeking for her to become what God has intended for her to be. He needs to be the Christian role model in her life. And as he, by his own life, demonstrates his love for her, then she will have a desire to please him. And with both husband and wife demonstrating love and submission, then Christ and His Church will be reflected in their marriage. This is the real goal for marriage.

Chapter V

Broken Marriages

Marriage should be a wonderful experience that lasts a lifetime. But sadly, for many it has been a heartbreaking experience that has been cut short by divorce. This is the one subject related to marriage about which I have no pleasure in writing.

You may not have experienced divorce in your immediate family, but it is almost certain that everyone has seen it in their extended families. It is also true that every church has had members who have gone through a divorce. And because it has touched our families and our churches, it is a very painful subject to discuss.

Another thing that makes it a difficult subject is the many different interpretations that there are. It is not my intention to discuss all the views on divorce and remarriage in this brief chapter. I am sure that I will not answer all the questions that you may have, and you may not agree with what I have to say on this subject. I know that I hold a very narrow view which is not popular with most people. But we all must stand on our convictions as we understand the Scriptures.

Jesus on Divorce

Let's begin by looking at what Jesus had to say about divorce. In the Sermon on the Mount, Jesus said,

"It hath been said, Whosoever shall put away his wife, let him give her a writing of divorcement: But I say unto

you, That whosoever shall put away his wife, saving for the cause of fornication, causeth her to commit adultery: and whosoever shall marry her that is divorced committeth adultery" (Matthew 5:31-32).

He first stated what seemed to be the general rule for the Jews of His day. Notice in verse 31 there is no reason given for the divorce. Then in verse 32, He says *"But I say unto you."*

He is addressing the subject of divorce with His authority instead of what others have said. He also puts a reason for divorce in His statement, *"saving for the cause of fornication."* So He is saying that when a man divorces his wife, he causes her to commit adultery and whoever marries her commits adultery. The only exception is if he divorces her because of fornication. Please notice, Jesus does not give her any grounds for remarriage.

Now let's listen to Jesus when the Pharisees tempting Him ask Him about divorce. Their question was,

"Is it lawful for a man to put away his wife for every cause?" (Matthew 19:3).

In other words, can he divorce her for any reason? Look at His answer,

"And he answered and said unto them, Have ye not read, that he which made them at the beginning made them male and female, And said, For this cause shall a man leave father and mother, and shall cleave to his wife: and they twain shall be one flesh? Wherefore they are no more twain, but one flesh. What therefore God hath joined together, let not man put asunder" (Matthew 19:4-6).

Please note how Jesus takes them back to Genesis and reminds them that two become one, and man is not to put asunder what God hath joined.

We have already seen how marriage binds and bonds a man and a woman together. And because of this binding and bonding where two become one, it is unnatural to break this union. The husband and wife have come together physically in a sexually intimate relationship. This relationship is such that God intended while the man and the woman are both alive, that they are to have no other partners in this sexual union. This is an element of marriage and divorce and remarriage that must not be overlooked.

The Pharisees, knowing the law, then asked Jesus,

"They say unto him, Why did Moses then command to give a writing of divorcement, and to put her away? He saith unto them, Moses because of the hardness of your hearts suffered you to put away your wives: but from the beginning it was not so" (Matthew 19:7-8).

Notice, they used the word "command," but Jesus told them Moses "suffered" or *permitted* them. Moses never commanded divorce; he simply was trying to regulate what was already going on. According to Jewish history, a man could divorce his wife by simply declaring it so verbally. Many times a woman was innocent yet she was divorced simply by a husband who just wanted another wife. So Moses gave instructions for a written divorce, in order to help protect innocent women. He permitted divorce, Jesus said, *"because of the hardness of your hearts."* But notice how Jesus ended that statement, *"but from the beginning it was not so"* (Matthew 19:8). Regardless of what Moses permitted, Jesus was saying that divorce was not a part of God's plan for man and woman. He used the phrase *"from the beginning,"* and in the beginning we see where one man and one woman are to become one flesh, emphasizing the unity and the oneness of the marriage relationship.

Regardless of our views about the reasons for divorce, we can assuredly say that there are no divorces that are pleasing to God! In Jesus' day there were Jews who followed the teaching of Shammai, who taught that a man could not divorce his wife unless it was for sexual immorality. Then there were those who followed Hillel, who allowed divorce for practically any reason.

Look now at what Jesus said about divorce,

"And I say unto you, Whosoever shall put away his wife, except it be for fornication, and shall marry another,

committeth adultery: and whoso marrieth her which is put away doth commit adultery" (Matthew 19:9).

Jesus said *"except it be for fornication."* He also used this word back in Matthew 5:32. So in both places He is teaching that fornication is the only grounds for a divorce. How one defines fornication will determine his view on grounds for divorce.

Fornication is the word that is usually used for sexual sins outside of marriage. We know that the Jews had a betrothal period before they were married. The betrothal period was binding, just like the marriage itself. A good example would be Joseph and Mary. When Joseph found out that Mary was pregnant, the Bible says,

"Then Joseph her husband, being a just man, and not willing to make her a publick example, was minded to put her away privily" (Matthew 1:19).

Joseph was going to "put away" his wife, Mary, which is another term for divorce. He thought that she had committed fornication.

Many people believe that when Jesus used the word *fornication*, He was permitting divorce in light of the Jewish custom concerning their betrothal period, but not after the marriage was consummated.

The word *fornication* is also used to describe all types of sexual sins including adultery, which is sexual sins of people that are married, sexual sins of the unmarried, homosexuality, and even bestiality. So, if Jesus was using the word in this light, then it would seem that He was permitting divorce on grounds of sexual immorality. But if so, remember it still is not God's will from the beginning.

The principle of two becoming one is a vital part of how you see divorce and remarriage. When a husband or a wife is untrue to his or her mate and commits sexual immorality, he or she has defiled not only himself or herself but also his or her spouse. An intimate relationship between the two has been broken, and now a third party has been involved, which is foreign to God's plan.

Let's consider the difference in what Jesus said about divorce in Matthew with what He said in Mark. In Matthew, Jesus only spoke of a man divorcing his wife. Under Jewish law a woman could not divorce her husband. It would seem then that Jesus had Jews in mind when He said what He did about divorce.

In Jesus' day, under Greek and Roman law, a woman could divorce her husband. We also know that the gospel of Mark was written with Gentiles in mind. So now look at what Jesus said about divorce:

"And he saith unto them, whosoever shall put away his wife, and marry another, committeth adultery against her. And if a woman shall put away her husband, and be married to another, she committeth adultery" (Mark 10:11-12).

Notice here in Mark's account there is no "except" clause for divorce like there is in Matthew. Also, here in Mark, He includes a woman putting away her husband, which He did not in Matthew. This statement in Mark seems to be directed more to Gentiles than what He said in Matthew. If we take His statement in Mark as directed to Gentiles, we would come to the conclusion that He permits no remarrying if a divorce takes place, because here He does not mention a permissible divorce. Again we go back to the fact that *"from the beginning it was not so."*

Paul, on Divorce and Remarriage

Let's read Paul's words to the church at Rome:

"Know ye not, brethren, (for I speak to them that know the law,) how that the law hath dominion over a man as long as he liveth? For the woman which hath an husband is bound by the law to her husband so long as he liveth; but if the husband be dead, she is loosed from the law of her husband. So then if, while her husband liveth, she be married to another man, she shall be called an adulteress: but if her husband be dead, she is free from that law; so that she is no adulteress, though she be married to another man" (Romans 7:1-3).

Of course we know that Paul was using this to teach that we are dead to the law that we might be married to Christ. But it does state Paul's understanding concerning marriage. It takes death to free a person in order to remarry.

It is my conviction that, even between those who are divorced, the death of one of the spouses is the only thing that frees a person to remarry. I know this seems hard and very narrow but, as we will continue to look at the Scriptures, we will see that Paul says nothing about remarriage for those divorced, yet he will state again that death frees one to remarry.

Writing to the church at Corinth about problems they were having concerning marriage, divorce and remarriage, Paul addresses believers,

"And unto the married I command, yet not I, but the Lord, Let not the wife depart from her husband: But and if she depart, let her remain unmarried, or be reconciled to her husband: and let not the husband put away his wife" (1 Corinthians 7:10-11).

He tells us in verse 10 that he is saying the same thing about marriage and divorce as the Lord, *"yet not I, but the Lord."* Notice that here he does not give any exceptions to what he is about to say. There are no grounds in divorce that permit a remarrying. Look again, *"if she depart, let her remain unmarried, or be reconciled to her husband."* Naturally, God's Will would be for reconciliation between the two. But if no reconciliation, there is to be no remarriage.

He then writes about a marriage between a believer and an unbeliever.

"And the woman which hath an husband that believeth not, and if he be pleased to dwell with her, let her not leave him. For the unbelieving husband is sanctified by the wife, and the unbelieving wife is sanctified by the husband: else were your children unclean; but now are they holy. But if the unbelieving depart, let him depart. A brother or a sister is not under bondage in such cases: but God hath called us to peace" (1 Corinthians 7:13-15).

Even in this case there is no mention of the freedom to remarry.

Paul then closes out the chapter on marriage with the only clear and stated grounds for remarriage.

"The wife is bound by the law as long as her husband liveth; but if her husband be dead, she is at liberty to be married to whom she will; only in the Lord" (1 Corinthians 7:39).

It seems to me that if divorce could free a person to remarry, then somewhere, Paul would have said so.

I know what people will say, "But what about the innocent person? Should he or she remain single when it wasn't his or her fault?" We all think that it does not seem fair.

Is it fair to the victim of murder? A life is cut short, when the person may have been totally innocent. Is it fair to a rape victim, to have to live with the emotional scars the rest of one's life? We live in a fallen world where there are a lot of things that do not seem fair. But we must trust God's wisdom in the laws and the guidelines that He has given us to live by.

I know that I do not have all the answers concerning divorce and remarriage. But this I do know – God can forgive sin if people are truly repentant about their sins, even if the divorce was because of their actions or was their choice. Divorce and remarriage is not God's will, but it is not the unpardonable sin.

I have known murderers, thieves, drunkards, and the like who found forgiveness with God. Did forgiveness undo their sins? Did it bring the dead back to life? Did it mend all the broken hearts? Did it take away the prison sentences? The answer is no.

So it is with divorce. Forgiveness may not change the past. It may not fix all the results of the broken marriage, but it can cleanse people of their sins. It can bring reconciliation between them and God. It can prepare them to live for God the rest of their lives.

We should never treat those who have gone through divorce and remarriage as second-class Christians. Those who are saved are as much a part of the family of God as anyone else. They can serve God in the local church and be a vital part of the Body of Christ.

I do believe that divorce and remarriage disqualifies a man from preaching or pastoring a church. It also disqualifies a man from serving as a deacon. And there will always be certain scars that people will have to bear because of a broken marriage. This is especially true where children are involved.

But if divorce and remarriage has taken place, the couple should seek God's forgiveness and strive to go on living for God and serve God in a local church.

Yes, God hates divorce, but remember, it may be your son, your daughter, or even yourself that may be part of a broken marriage. How would you treat your own children? Will you stop loving them? Will you isolate yourself from them? I don't think so. And God is not going to give up on His children either.

Do not think that I am saying that we are to take this lightly, because we shouldn't. As a church we are to preach and to practice God's Word on this. We should train our people about a Biblical marriage. We should never silence our voices about the truth because we may have people in our congregations who have had failed marriages. But we should preach in love and not intentionally seek to push couples further down.

Truly, divorce is always a painful subject to talk about. There will always be different views as to the grounds of divorce and the freedom to remarry. But I believe that we all can agree that divorce was not a part of God's original plan, and it is not His Will for any of us today.

Every marriage will have times of testing and trials when it seems like the only thing to do is to divorce. This is the easy way out. We know that it takes both spouses to make a marriage work; so one person alone cannot keep the marriage together. But God's will is for a husband and a wife to work through their problems and to do everything in their power to have a good marriage.

If we are to preserve Biblical marriage in our society, then we must maintain a high standard and what many may call a narrow view when it comes to divorce and remarriage. We must teach and then set an example before our young people that marriage is still a holy union between a man and a woman, and that it is to be a life-long commitment.

As I have already stated, half of all marriages will end in divorce. We must do more as Christians, especially as church leaders, to reach out to and to minister to people in their marriage relationships. Regardless of whether you are in a first marriage or a second marriage, God's Will is for you first of all to have a right relationship with Him, and then to have a right relationship with your spouse.

If you have had the unpleasant experience of a failed marriage, then you must go on with your life. You can seek God's forgiveness in the areas of sin and failure and then trust His grace for the future.

Regardless of our past, God is able to set before us a path that will be pleasing to Him and a blessing to us. But we must seek the teaching of the Word of God concerning this path.

In closing, we must be reminded that God instituted marriage. We must seek His Will and His Word if we want to have a Biblical marriage. And then, when it is all over we will give an account of ourselves to Christ at the Judgment Seat. We, as husbands and wives, and as parents, will be held accountable to God for our lives. So we should be motivated, not only by this life but also for eternity, to be who God wants us to be.

Bringing Up Children

Part Two

Chapter VI

The Blessings of Bringing Up Children

In his writings to the church of Ephesus about parental responsibility, The Apostle Paul writes,

"And, ye fathers, provoke not your children to wrath: but bring them up in the nurture and admonition of the Lord" (Ephesians 6:4).

From this verse I have taken a key phrase for the text in this second part of the book. Please note, "bring them up." Using this as our text, we will consider Bringing Up Children.

In this chapter we will consider the **Blessings** of bringing up children. The Word of God gives us several natural and spiritual blessings that are a result of bringing up children according to the Scriptures.

1. Fulfilling Man's Responsibility of Replenishing the Earth.

In Genesis 1:28 we read,

"And God blessed them, and God said unto them, Be fruitful, and multiply, and replenish the earth, and subdue it: and have dominion over the fish of the sea, and over the fowl of the air, and over every living thing that moveth upon the earth."

The word *replenish* simply means "to fill." God was telling men and women to bear children in order to populate the earth. God could have created as many people as He wanted in the beginning, but He chose to create only one man, Adam, and then from Adam's rib, God made Eve.

And from the union of Adam and Eve, as children began to be born, the process of filling the earth was under way. This was God's sovereign design, and when husbands and wives bring children into the world, they are fulfilling a God–given responsibility.

Those who deny a Divine creation and hold to the theory of evolution would also fail to realize this blessing of fulfilling God's will. I also believe that there is a connection between people believing in evolution and how they view the value and worth of children. For example, if people believe that we are a product of the evolutionary process, then it will be easier for them to accept abortion. But if people believe the Genesis account of creation and the charge that God gave mankind about bringing children into the world, then it will be easier for them to see abortion as it is: the murder of the unborn child.

God blessed Carolyn and me with two daughters, Jennifer and Keisha. It is a real blessing to know that you have been a part of God's plan when you see your children in the light of God's command *to replenish the earth.*

2. The Fruit of the Marriage Union

In the book of Psalms we read,

"Lo, children are an heritage of the LORD: and the fruit of the womb is his reward" (Psalm 127:3).

We are looking at the words, *"the fruit of the womb."* To understand why God uses the word *fruit* to illustrate the birth of a child, let us consider a fruit tree. In the spring time we see fruit trees blooming. We also know that bees will go from tree to tree collecting nectar from the blossoms, and in so doing they pollinate the fruit trees, a process of fertilization. We also must have the same process for most of our garden plants. So the fruit then becomes a product of the fertilization.

In our text then, the fruit of the womb is used to describe how a baby that is born is the fruit of the physical union between a husband and a wife. Just like the fruit tree, there must be fertilization. A child is a tangible result of the two becoming one.

I remember how I felt when our two daughters were born. Carolyn and I were husband and wife, and now because of our marriage union, we held in our arms the fruit of that union.

When children are seen in this light, it will help to further **bind the hearts** of the husband and wife together when they realize that they, according to God's plan, have brought life into the world, a life that did not exist before their union.

Children not only help to bind the couple, but they also are given to us to help **mature** us as husband and wife. I know it is the parents' responsibility to help mature their children, but let's face it, we as parents learn so much and no doubt mature ourselves by having our children to raise.

A husband no longer sees his wife as just a wife, but now he sees her as the mother of their child. The wife no longer sees just her husband, but the father of their child. So having children brings the man and woman into a new experience with each other that they did not have in the past. This is why it is a blessing to bring up children. The parents are benefited in so many ways by their own personal growth and by growth in the relationship to one another.

The fruit of the womb also **satisfies** the inborn desire of a woman to have a child. In I Samuel we read of Hannah and her prayer to God for a child.

> *"And she was in bitterness of soul, and prayed unto the Lord, and wept sore. And she vowed a vow, and said, O Lord of hosts, if thou wilt indeed look on the affliction of thine handmaid, and remember me, and not forget thine handmaid, but wilt give unto thine handmaid a man child, then I will give him unto the Lord all the days of his life, and there shall no razor come upon his head"* (1 Samuel 1:10-11).

Hannah was grieved that she could not have a child, and this was the purpose of her prayer. We see the same attitude among different women throughout the Bible. A Jewish woman felt cheated and even cursed if she could not have a baby.

We all have seen how natural it is for a little girl to play with dolls. They don't even have to be shown how to treat them. God has put in the heart of even a little girl the natural desire of motherhood. But sadly, in this wicked and perverted society, girls are taught by liberals the philosophy of the feminist movement. This world with its opposition to God would tell young women that motherhood is second class. They are told that they should seek fulfillment in their careers, that having children will just be a hindrance to their personal happiness.

I am not against women having a career or, along with their husband, deciding to limit the number of children they will have. But I am against the teachings of the trends of our day that are influencing women to forsake their God-given place in the home as it relates to their husbands and to their children.

While many women have an abortion to end an undesirable pregnancy, there are many women who are unable to have a child.

3. The Future of Our Families

Let's read what is said of Adam:

"And Adam lived an hundred and thirty years, and begat a son in his own likeness, after his image; and called his name Seth: And the days of Adam after he had begotten Seth were eight hundred years: and he begat sons and daughters: And all the days that Adam lived were nine hundred and thirty years: and he died. And Seth lived an hundred and five years, and begat Enos" (Genesis 5:3-6).

We know that Adam was the first man and that Eve the first woman. Their first two sons were Cain and Abel, and we know that Cain killed Abel. But now, with the birth of Seth in chapter five, we can trace Adam's family all the way to Noah. This is a chapter that repeatedly says, *"and he died."* It shows us that we must all go by way of death unless we are alive when the rapture takes place.

But it is also a chapter of hope, for we see the continuation of Adam's family through the birth of children. Simply put, bringing children into the world extends our family.

The real blessing comes when you understand the sovereignty of God in it all. For example, let's consider the genealogy of Jesus. Matthew traces Jesus back to Abraham through Joseph, His legal (though not natural) father. Matthew seeks to show that Jesus has a legal right to David's throne as an heir of David.

We then see His ancestry in Luke through the genealogy of Mary, His mother. Here Jesus is traced all the way back to Adam, to show that He truly is the son of man.

The truth that I want you to see is that every person in Jesus' genealogy was a link in the chain that brought Him into the world. So in this light, we should realize that we, and the children that we bring into the world, are always a part of what God is going to do in the future.

We could list a great host of famous people who have lived and made a great impact on this world. But if we did, who would know the names of their parents or grandparents? Regardless of who we could mention, most people would not know their families before them. So it is now. In God's providence none of us know what God can and will do with our children or grandchildren or even in generations to come.

But in God's plan, it is important to be a link in the chain of His Sovereign design. I hope you can see the blessings that are involved, as children are the future of our families.

4. The Friends of Jesus

I believe that children have a special place in the heart of Jesus. As we read the gospels, we can see the love and affection that He showed them.

"And they brought young children to him, that he should touch them: and his disciples rebuked those that brought them. But when Jesus saw it, he was much displeased, and said unto them, Suffer the little children to come unto me, and forbid them not: for of such is the kingdom of God. Verily I say unto you, Whosoever shall not receive the kingdom of God as a little child, he shall not enter therein. And he took them up in his arms, put his hands upon them, and blessed them" (Mark 10:13-16).

Indeed, when a person gets saved, he or she must be as humble as a child and also as trusting as a child. Little children usually have not developed a prideful attitude like adults. God does not want adults to be childish, but there are traits of children that we should have.

In our text, the disciples thought that these children would be in the way or that they would bother Jesus. It displeased Him for them to think this way. He then took them up in His arms and blessed them.

Let's look now at what Matthew recorded about Jesus and children:

"At the same time came the disciples unto Jesus, saying, Who is the greatest in the kingdom of heaven? And Jesus called a little child unto him, and set him in the midst of them, And said, Verily I say unto you, Except ye be converted, and become as little children, ye shall not enter into the kingdom of heaven. Whosoever therefore shall humble himself as this little child, the same is greatest in the kingdom of heaven. And whoso shall receive one such little child in my name receiveth me. But whoso shall offend one of these little ones which believe in me, it were better for him that a millstone were hanged about his neck, and that he were drowned in the depth of the sea" (Matthew 18:1-6).

Here we see basically the same thing. Jesus is pointing out the humility of a child. However, here He adds two things. In verse 5 he says, *"and whoso shall receive one such little child in my name receiveth me."* This speaks volumes on how we should treat children. It tells us how dear to the heart of God children are.

He also gave a warning in verse 6 about anyone offending a little child. It grieves us to hear about someone abusing a child, and I say they should be punished for it. But in light of these Scriptures, can you imagine how Jesus feels when He looks down on earth and sees all that goes on today?

Children suffer sexual abuse, physical abuse, and mental abuse, and also are deprived of spiritual opportunities. We know that millions have been killed in abortions. Surely, the judgment of God must already be upon us as a nation for our sins against children, the friends of Jesus.

Another verse tells us of the special place children have with God.

"Take heed that ye despise not one of these little ones; for I say unto you, That in heaven their angels do always behold the face of my Father which is in heaven" (Matthew 18:10).

I believe this means just what it says, that there are angels always beholding the face of God on the behalf of children. Just think – angels in God's presence, on behalf of little children!

As we see what the Bible says about Jesus and children, it should enlighten our eyes as to the privilege and the responsibility that we have as parents and also as a church.

God surely is paying attention as to how children are being raised in our homes. Knowing this, every parent should seek to find out from the Word of God how He expects us to bring up our children. After all, the standard by which He has given us to live will be the standard by which we will be judged.

Churches should do everything they can, according to Scripture, to reach children with the gospel message. And when they are saved, we should train and teach them how to live a godly life as they grow into adulthood.

Little children are the friends of Jesus, and He has entrusted them to us for their care. May God help us to do our best as unto the Lord.

Chapter VII

Beginning with an Understanding

As we begin to study the Scriptures that teach us how to bring up children, I believe it is necessary for us to start by understanding and knowing exactly the situation our children are in. When we understand them and what they are faced with, then we can have a better sense of direction in our training of them.

1. The Opposition Children Face

As you hold a newborn baby in your arms, it's hard to imagine that this little baby could have any enemies. They come into this world so innocent, so sweet and loving. Yet, these little ones grow up to be adults that may become thieves, drunkards, murderers, and any other term that describe a sinful lifestyle. The question is then asked, "What happens that a child could go from being so sweet and innocent to being so cruel and wicked?" You may be surprised, but the Bible gives us the answer.

First of all, the Bible teaches that every child is born with the Adamic nature or, as we call it, **the sin nature**. In Genesis 5:3 we read,

"And Adam lived an hundred and thirty years, and begat a son in his own likeness, after his image; and called his name Seth."

Notice the phrase, *"in his own likeness, after his image."* This is exactly how each one of us came into the world. This sin nature is the greatest problem and opposition that a child will face.

In Romans 3:10-12 we read of the condition of all people, *"As it is written, there is none righteous, no not one."*

This is the **sinner's position.** The Scripture goes on to say, *"There is none that understandeth, there is none that seeketh after God."*

This is the **sinner's perception**. And finally we read, *"They are all gone out of the way, they are together become unprofitable, there is none that doeth good, no not one."*

This is the **sinner's practice.**

This does not just describe adults, but it is true of children, also. This does not mean that children are wicked as to their actions, but it does mean that they have a nature that is fallen and, if left to themselves, they will walk after the influence of their sin nature.

In Proverbs 29:15 we read,

"The rod and reproof give wisdom: but a child left to himself bringeth his mother to shame." This is why a child's greatest opposition is his sinful nature.

Even as an adult, my greatest challenge is dealing with my own sinful nature. So as parents we must recognize the fact that these sweet little children have a natural bent toward evil. Children do not have to be taught to do wrong; that comes naturally for them. But they do have to be taught to do right.

Understanding that your child has a spiritual problem will help you to seek spiritual help for your child. The most important thing you can do for your children is to live the Christian life before them and to teach them about the things of God, so that when they reach the age of accountability, they will also trust Jesus Christ as their Lord and Saviour.

When someone gets saved, they become partakers of the Divine nature. This is our only hope of overcoming our sin nature. Paul makes this clear in Galatians 5:16 when he writes,

"This I say then walk in the Spirit, and ye shall not fulfill the lust of the flesh."

The flesh of course is another term for the sin nature or the Adamic nature. And this sin nature is one of the sources of temptation.

"But every man is tempted, when he is drawn away of his own lust, and enticed" (James 1:14).

We are to train our children, we are to keep them in church, and we should try to shelter them from as much of the world as we can. But the fact is that your child is a sinner by nature, and he or she needs God in his or her life.

Secondly, children face opposition from the **world**. By the world, I mean this world's ideas, practices, and just the way people live in opposition to the ways of God. John writes,

> *"Love not the world, neither the things that are in the world. If any man love the world, the love of the Father is not in him. For all that is in the world, the lust of the flesh, and the lust of the eyes, and the pride of life, is not of the Father, but is of the world"* (1 John 2:15-16).

The reason the world has such a pull on us is because of our fallen nature. The world's system is basically people living out their lives after the desires of their sin nature.

This is another reason why a child cannot be left to himself or herself. Children are faced with the opposition and the pull of this sinful society. They are exposed to it on television, on the radio, in the shopping malls, and certainly at school.

It is sad to think about what small children will have to face as they are growing up. There are drugs, sexual temptations, rebellion to parents and others in authority, and homosexuality and same-sex marriage.

There is also a worldly view of Christianity to which they will be exposed. In public schools and in secular universities their faith will be challenged. They will hear the attacks on the Word of God and old-time worship. They will be criticized if they hold to Biblical standards concerning morals.

I graduated from high school in 1975, and I know that I did not have to face as much as children and young people face today. It takes courage and convictions for young people to stand for God in these days. Parents truly have their jobs cut out for them in bringing up children in today's society.

Paul wrote,

"And be not conformed to this world: but be ye transformed by the renewing of your mind, that ye may prove what is that good, and acceptable, and perfect will of God" (Romans 12:2).

The word *conformed* means that this world seeks to shape our lives after its standards and pattern, but we are to resist this. We are to be *transformed*, which means we are to be changed from within, we are to be made in the image of Jesus Christ.

This needs to be the goal of all parents: to seek to do all they can to keep this world from shaping their children, and to do their best to bring them up in the nurture and the admonition of the Lord.

Thirdly, we also know that children are opposed by **Satan**.

"Be sober, be vigilant; because your adversary the devil, as a roaring lion, walketh about, seeking whom he may devour" (I Peter 5:8).

Have you ever thought about the fact that in the Bible there is never a certain age at which the devil targets a person?

We may think that he is considerate and does not trouble children, but this is not the case. He is seeking whom he may devour, regardless of age. His whole purpose is to oppose God and His program for mankind. Anything that he can do to hinder, he will do it.

In the gospels there were occasions when children were demon possessed or under demonic influence. Some of Israel's kings began to reign as teenagers and were certainly targets of Satan's attacks.

It was the Serpent, or Satan, who tempted Eve in the garden. It was Satan who tempted Jesus in the wilderness. And it is Satan who desires to destroy our children, just to hinder the work of God by attacking children who will grow up to be a vital part of the Kingdom of God.

Always remember, Satan is a liar and a murderer (John 8:44). Your child will face his lies. He or she will face Satan as a murderer who will try to destroy them.

I know these are strong words, but please do not underestimate the devil's power and his pursuit to destroy lives.

Now, let's begin to look at all three of these things that children face, in light of each other. They are opposed by their own flesh, by the world, and by Satan. Here is the real problem parents have to deal with. First of all, a child is born with a fallen nature, with a bent toward evil. Secondly, this child lives in a society, in a world that is fallen, where the influence to sin is everywhere, where most people around him or her live with no restraints concerning sin. Then finally on top of this, the devil and his demons are engaged in spiritual warfare against the child or young person. The devil will take the things of this world and present them to the child, appealing to his sin nature. So children, young people, and adults as well, are constantly bombarded with the pressure of all three. No wonder people's lives are ruined! It is only by the grace of God that anyone lives victorious in today's society.

This, mom and dad, is what you are up against. You need to understand your child and the opposition that he or she faces in order to bring your child up as unto the Lord.

2. A Time of Opportunity

Every parent should also understand that childhood is a Time of Opportunity.

I am told that the first two to three years of a child's life are among the most important. It will be during these early years that his or her foundation for learning is laid down. So as parents and also as a church it is important to understand the great opportunity we have during this time of children's lives. This truth is seen in Proverbs 22:6,

"Train up a child in the way he should go: and when he is old, he will not depart from it."

Notice the two time periods in a person's life; one is "a child" and the other is when "he is old." It is during the time when one is a child that God tells us to train him or her, and then this training will affect his or her life thereafter.

I know everyone is concerned about their children getting a good education. We want them to take advantage of their youth and to get all the education necessary for them to be able to earn a living for themselves and for their own families.

But it is more important to see the time of their youth as an opportunity to teach them the ways of God. I will deal with the parents' responsibilities later, but for now let me emphasize the importance of understanding the time element that is involved.

We all know that as we get older, we become more set in our ways. We develop a pattern of habits. We settle into a way of reasoning and a way of decision making.

But a child's heart and mind are very impressionable. It is like the illustration of the potter and the clay. The potter works with the clay while it is fresh and moist. But as the clay hardens, it is harder to shape. So it is in a person's life. It is so important to teach children about God, His Will, and His Word for their lives while they are tender, while it can make a lasting impression on them.

Children are never too young to bring to church, never too young to attend Sunday school. In our church we have a nursery for babies, but I like for the rest of the children to be in the worship service with the adults. I believe it is important for children, even though they may be only two or three years old, to witness their parents and others in worship of God.

It is amazing how much a little one will hear and understand about the preaching and the singing. This is a vital part of laying the right foundation for them spiritually. Usually children who are raised in church from infants will come to Christ at an early age.

At home, parents should take the time to read Bible stories to their young children. They should also pray with them. I still remember that when I was a child, my mother would tuck us into bed and always help us to say the little bedtime prayer. It is things like this that will stick with a child.

Children grow up so fast. This means that parents have very little time to make the most of those childhood days. Yes, they can learn as teenagers, they can continue to learn throughout their lives. But those early years, even as a toddler, are going to be the most critical in teaching your child. So let us reach out and minister to them in their days of opportunity.

3. Days of Obligation

Childhood days should also be days of obligation. By this I mean that even little children should be taught responsibility at their own level.

Mothers and fathers should teach their children that they also have obligations and that they are going to have responsibilities. A child even two years of age should be trained to put his or her toys away. This is simple, not a big deal, but it teaches a child responsibility. Yes, it is so much easier for mom and dad to do everything for their little one. Most would rather just do it themselves than try to train their children to do it.

But in doing it for them, you *are* training them. You are teaching them that if they put up a fuss, they can get out of work. These are the things that children learn that will be the basis for their thinking.

I thank God that my mother and father made us do things around the house. I had to work in the chicken house and in the garden. They taught us that we had to fulfill the responsibilities that were given to us. This is just a good work ethic. This principle of fulfilling one's obligations is carried into every area of life. And as parents we need to understand this. We need to understand that children must be held accountable to their obligations. Understanding this will help you to see the importance of your job in training them.

Solomon wrote,

"Remember now thy Creator in the days of thy youth" (Ecclesiastes 12:1a).

Children should also be taught about their obligations to God. Even before a child gets saved, he or she should be taught that we are responsible for our lives and for the decisions we make about God.

Listen to what Solomon said,

"Let us hear the conclusion of the whole matter: Fear God and keep his commandments: for this is the whole duty of man. For God shall bring every work into judgment, with every secret thing, whether it be good, or whether it be evil" (Ecclesiastes 12:13-14).

Solomon said this was the conclusion of the whole matter. He looked at life with all of its experiences and summed it up by saying two basic things: (1) we have a responsibility to keep God's commandments; and (2) we will have to give an account to God for our lives.

This is what I am trying to say about understanding the obligations that our children have. They are responsible and they will be held accountable. This should help us as parents to be more serious about bringing up children.

The book of Proverbs has much to say about a child's obligations. In 1:8 we read,

"My son, hear the instruction of thy father, and forsake not the law of thy mother." Also in 4:1 it says, *"Hear, ye children, the instruction of a father, and attend to know understanding."*

Again in 6:20 we read,

"My son, keep thy father's commandment, and forsake not the law of thy mother."

These are just a few of the verses which teach that children have an obligation to their parents and to God. Understanding this principle gives parents the foundation for training and for disciplining their children.

There is much said today about the child's rights. But don't let the world tell you how to raise your children. It is neither the government's nor society's responsibility. It is the parents' job and privilege.

May God help this generation to use the Word of God as a guidebook on raising children. May we as Christians set the example for others to follow.

As I conclude this chapter, let me state again that we should begin with understanding: understanding the opposition children face; understanding childhood as days of opportunity; and understanding that children have obligations to God and to parents.

Chapter VIII

Bible Principles
For Bringing up Children

In this chapter we will consider Paul's instructions for parenting found in the book of Ephesians 6:1-4. We will look at three things:

1. Parental Authority (6:1-3)
2. Parental goals (6:4)
3. Parental Responsibility (6:4)

1. Parental Authority

Paul is writing about different relationships in chapters 5 and 6. In chapter 5, he shows us the relationship between a husband and a wife and how this pictures the relationship between Christ and the Church. In chapter 6, he writes about the parent-child relationship and also the relationship between masters and slaves.

As Christians we are to use our position in Christ and the change that it makes in our lives, in all the different relationships we have. As Paul begins chapter 6, he gives instructions to children.

"Children, obey your parents in the Lord: for this is right. Honour thy father and mother; (which is the first commandment with promise;) That it may be well with thee, and thou mayest live long on the earth." (Ephesians 6:1-3).

The command for children to obey implies **Parental Authority**. The key word in this command is *obey*. The

Greek word is *Hupakouo*. It comes from two words. The first is *hupo* which means "under," and the second is *akouo*, which means "to hear." Thus the meaning is "to listen and to submit; to hear under authority."

God is a God of order. We have already seen this in the order established between a husband and a wife. We now see that God is putting the children under the authority of their parents. This principle is to be one of the first things that a child should come to realize as he or she begins to understand, even as a baby.

Parents should establish early with their children who is in authority. It is sad to see a child lead his father and mother around as though he was in control.

As small and as young as children may be, they still know how to test their parents. They soon learn how to manipulate them in getting their way. It may be by crying, pouting, or just pitching a "mad fit," but they will test mom and dad. And if mom and dad give in, then the child has learned a bad lesson for life.

How a child views and understands authority will be with him or her for life. A child who gives problems at school or a young person who has problems with those in authority, most often does not have a right relationship with his or her parents. This is why it is so important as parents to understand what God expects of us in this area. If we fail with our children while they are small, then we are teaching them to be rebels, to ignore rules, and to show no respect for those in authority.

As a parent, you just cannot compromise on this subject. You will have to be tough and firm. But at the same time, you must discipline in love, letting the child know that it is because you love him or her and it is for his or her benefit that you are in charge and he or she is going to have to obey you!

Paul said for children to *"obey your parents in the Lord: for this is right."* Simply put, it is just the right thing to do. But children must be taught this by their parents.

Let's consider now Ephesians 6:2,

"Honour thy father and mother; (which is the first commandment with promise)."

And what is this promise? *"That it may be well with thee, and thou mayest live long on the earth."* Paul is quoting the fifth commandment that God gave Israel in Exodus 20:12.

The word *honour* implies "to estimate or to fix the value." It implies that we are to recognize the value that God puts upon parents. For a child to honour his parents means that he is recognizing his own submission to his parents as well as the benefit and the value that his parents bring to him.

If a child at an early age learns how to obey and to honor his parents, then he will understand how to submit to and to honor God.

Under the Mosaic Law, Jewish parents could have a rebellious child stoned to death. Yes, this is harsh, and I am not condoning physical child abuse, but this does tell us the importance that God puts on parental authority.

Paul, in writing to Timothy about the Last Days, said that children *"would be disobedient to parents"* (II Timothy 3:2). Truly we are seeing this fulfilled before our very eyes.

Writing about people who God had given over to a reprobate mind, Paul said that one of the results would be, *"disobedient to parents"* (Romans 1:30).

Parents should understand that this is not just a natural family problem between parents and children, but that is also a spiritual problem as well. Parents are in God's order of authority for the home, and the blessing of God will only be upon the children as they submit and obey their parents in the Lord.

Every parent should realize that rebellious children grow up to be rebellious adults. God is the only one who can break and control this rebellion. But He uses parents equipped with the Word of God to be the agents in His hand.

If you have a child or children, then let me ask, "Who is in authority in your home?" You must be the parent. You must exercise your God-given authority over your children.

2. Parental Goals

We now turn our attention to Ephesians 6:4,

"And, ye fathers, provoke not your children to wrath: but bring them up in the nurture and admonition of the Lord."

The phrase *bring them up* means "to nourish up to maturity." Simply put, parents are to take care of, to teach, and to train a child from the time of his or her birth until he or she reaches adulthood.

In doing this, parents should have a plan or what I call "certain goals" that they want to achieve in bringing up their children. I want us to consider four areas of a child's development in which every parent should be seeking to help the child to mature.

For our text we will look at Jesus as our example.

"And he went down with them, and came to Nazareth, and was subject unto them: but his mother kept all these sayings in her heart. And Jesus increased in wisdom and stature, and in favour with God and man" (Luke 2:51-52).

At this time Jesus was twelve years old. We have very little record of the childhood days of Jesus, but what we do have provides us with great insight into His submission and obedience to Mary and Joseph.

One of the great mysteries is the incarnation – God became a man. To think, God became a baby, grew up in this world as any other boy, and submitted Himself to Joseph and Mary. But verse 52 gives us an amazing statement. It tells us that Jesus *"increased in wisdom and stature, and in favour with God and man."* In this statement we see four areas of development that all parents should have as goals for their children.

Intellectually

First consider that Jesus increased in wisdom. I know that there is a difference between knowledge and wisdom, but here let's combine the two and think of them both as being included in the word *intellectually.*

All parents should have as a goal the intellectual growth and development of their children. I cannot imagine anyone not wanting his or her child to have a good education. As time has changed, we live in a far more advanced world than it use to be. In today's workplace a college education or some special training is almost necessary in order to get a good job. A good education will begin at home. The basic ideas of learning should be taught by the parents before the child ever starts to school. The discipline to study should be instilled in the child by the parents.

I am afraid we have come to depend on the government far too much, including for the education of our children. Private schools and home schooling have become a great alternative for many parents. But the greatest lessons in life will be those taught by moms and dads at home. For your child to develop intellectually, he will need a combination of academics and lessons on life that only a home environment can provide.

One thing you can't learn in a classroom setting is common sense. This is where wisdom comes in. I have known a lot of great people who may have lacked for more education, but they were intellectual giants. They seemed to have an understanding of what life is all about, and by applying common sense and hard work, they were great achievers in life, whether it was in the Lords' work or in secular occupations.

The point I am trying to make is that parents should make it a goal in their parenting to see that their children have every opportunity possible to prepare them for their lives.

Physically

In Luke 2:52 we also find the word *stature*. Jesus not only increased in wisdom, but also in stature. The word *stature* comes from a word that basically means "age." From this we can see that Jesus increased physically as he grew older until adulthood. The second goal we should have is to see our children grow up to physical maturity. To increase intellectually is for the mind; to increase physically is for the body.

There are three basic things that parents can do for their children concerning their physical growth: diet, exercise, and proper medical attention. Briefly let's consider these.

I believe everyone knows the importance of a healthy diet. But the problem is making sure children eat the right foods. The best way to achieve this is for the whole family to develop healthy eating habits. Given the choice, a child will always choose sweets and junk food over vegetables and meats. Children should not be given this choice. I am not saying to never give them any sweets, candy, or the like, but you, the parent, should make sure they have good, balanced meals. Too often I have seen parents give in to their children's whining about what they want to eat. Good eating habits can be learned and will greatly benefit the child in his or her development.

The second thing that is important to physical development is exercise. When I was growing up, we didn't have computers or video games. Most all of our playing was outside. I grew up in the country, so we were always out in the woods or running in the yard. We got plenty of good fresh air and exercise. Then as we got older, my brother and I helped in the garden and worked in the chicken houses with my father and mother.

As I look back on those years, I am thankful that we were made to get out and work. It not only taught us a good work ethic, but it was physically good for us.

Your child may be involved in sports and, in so doing, he or she is receiving good exercise. But if not, see to it that he or she gets out of the house and gets some exercise. Give your children responsibilities around the house that involve some physical labor, some "hands on" experience. It will not only be physically good for them, but it will help them to develop some common sense as well.

Thirdly, parents should provide their children with the proper medical attention they need. This may be as simple as check-ups, or it may involve treatments for specific problems. With all the medical care available in America today, there is no excuse for children not receiving good medical attention. Our goal should be to do whatever we can do to ensure that our children have every opportunity to grow and to mature physically.

Spiritually

Our text in Luke 2:52 also says that Jesus increased in *"favour with God."* This describes His spiritual relationship to the Father.

As we look at Jesus in His growing years as an example for children today, we see Him developing spiritually. So from this, we see our third goal for our children as we *"bring them up."*

We should strive to have a balance in the development of our children. We should be concerned for their intellectual growth, for their physical growth, and also for their spiritual growth. Sadly, this is an area where many parents fail to be concerned. They do everything to see that they receive a good education to prepare them intellectually for the future, but they fail to help prepare them spiritually.

Spiritual training must begin when children are young and their hearts are tender. Usually, if a child has been in church, under good Bible teaching and preaching, he or she will come to Christ at an early age. This should be the most important goal that parents have for their children. I remember well when our two daughters were born into the family of God. What a blessing and a relief it was. The new birth marked the beginning of their spiritual journey. And moms and dads should do everything in their power to see that their children have every opportunity to grow in their faith.

A word of caution is in order here. Parents should be careful not to push their children into a decision for Christ until the children are ready. And by ready I mean under Holy Ghost conviction. Salvation is more than a mental decision and a simple prayer. It is a birth from above. It takes the Spirit of God to convict and also to convert a person. God must do the saving in His time, not ours. So be patient and do not press a decision out of their minds when it is not in their hearts.

One of the best ways to help train your child is by example. Mothers and fathers should live godly Christian lives before their children. They should show them what a Christian is and not just tell them what one is.

Parents should be sure that they are in a good fundamental Bible-preaching church where their children will be exposed to sound teaching and preaching and to good Christian principles by which to live. As a Pastor, I often get calls from parents asking what type of programs we have for the young people. They don't ask about what Bible we use or about our Sunday school or our missions programs. They don't ask about our worship service and what kind of preaching I do.

I must confess that I come from the "old school." I think the Word of God taught in Sunday school and the Word of God preached by the under-shepherd of the flock, which includes the lambs (children), is a pretty good youth program.

We do a disservice to our children when we take them out of our worship service and put them by themselves. I believe they need to see mom and dad worshipping. I believe they need that experience even though they are small.

Yes, we do provide a nursery for those who want to put their babies there or for those who may need to give them special attention, but our children are in the worship service with the adults.

I could say a whole lot more here, but before I leave this subject, let me say this to all the moms and dads. You only have one chance at raising your children. You will not get a second chance. They will grow from babies to adults. They are your responsibility to "bring up."

Socially

Our text also says that Jesus increased in favour "with man." We can look at this as developing social skills: the ability to interact with others, to have relationship skills.

Every child has his or her own personality. Some will be more outgoing than others, while some will be shy by nature. This is something you can't change. But you can help them to learn the basic skills needed to interact. Again this should be part of this four-fold goal that all parents should have for their children. This will help your child to be well-balanced as he or she reaches adulthood.

I believe the best way to acquire social skills is by experience itself. Parents should demonstrate good relationship qualities to their children. Children should be able to learn by example how to be kind, courteous, and considerate of others. This should be demonstrated in conversation, in manners, and even in business dealings. Parents should observe closely how their children act around other children and with adults as well. They should be quick to deal with any undesirable behavior by their children. Again, this is to be taught by the parents.

Something as simple as teaching a child to share his toys is part of learning social skills. Teaching children to respect adults and people in authority will help them develop attitudes they will have the rest of their lives.

Husbands and wives should be aware of how they treat each other in front of their children. In reality you are giving your children a lesson on how to treat their future spouses. Sadly all lessons are not good lessons. Children will learn the bad as well as the good.

So let me encourage you to think about the relationship skills that you are teaching your child, consciously or unconsciously.

In summary, from Ephesians 6:4 we are told to *"bring them up,"* which means "to nourish up to maturity." Parents should set goals for bringing their children to maturity, for seeing them develop *Intellectually*, *Physically*, *Spiritually*, and *Socially*.

3. Parental Responsibility

From Ephesians 6:4 we have already looked at Parental Authority and Parental Goals. Now I would like for us to consider Parental Responsibility. It is obvious that under the first two subjects we have already considered a lot of the responsibility that parents have in bringing up children. But I would like for us to consider some words in our text and look a bit deeper at our responsibility.

Again our text says,

"And, ye fathers, provoke not you children to wrath: but bring them up in the nurture and admonition of the Lord" (Ephesians 6:4).

We have already considered *bring them up* or to "nourish to maturity," under Parental goals.

In The Nurture: The Greek word for nurture is *paideia*, which means "the training of a child, including instruction, discipline, and correction." What we find here is the means by which we achieve the goals that we set for bringing up our children. We are to use training, instruction, and discipline when necessary.

And Admonition: The Greek word for admonition is *nouthesia*, which means "a putting in the mind." It is the training by word, whether of encouragement or, if necessary, by reproof.

We will consider our responsibility from these two words. God expects us to train our children. This training is to be in the form of instruction and also of discipline, which carries the idea of correction.

Let's look now in the book of Proverbs at some verses that tell us a great deal about instruction and correction.

"Train up a child in the way he should go: and when he is old, he will not depart from it" (Proverbs 22:6).

Let's think about the word *train*. The Hebrew word for *train* means "to dedicate, the setting aside, it speaks of a narrowing or a hedging in." To train a child then means to narrow in or to hedge in the path that they are taking.

The word *way* in verse 6 means "a proper way, path of wise or path of wisdom." So as we train our children, we are trying to start them on a narrow way or path. Remember Jesus' words:

> *"Enter ye in at the strait gate: for wide is the gate, and broad is the way, that leadeth to destruction, and many there be which go in thereat: Because strait is the gate, and narrow is the way, which leadeth unto life, and few there be that find it"* (Matthew 7:13-14).

The world offers a broad way and a wide gate. It is easy to take this route of no convictions, of no standards, with the idea that everything is okay. The world's idea is of being tolerant, or as many see it, as having no absolute truths. But this way leads to destruction. So in training children you are trying to narrow down the path, to hedge them in. This means you establish convictions and standards.

It means that you have to put up barriers in their lives and, when they cross those barriers, there is pain associated with it. I know this is a very crude illustration, but consider this. Many people who have dogs have an electric wire around their yard. The dogs have shock collars on. If the dog gets near the wire, the collar will warn him with a light tingle; then if the dog crosses the wire he gets a shock he won't forget. It doesn't take but a time or two until he learns to take heed to the warning. What you have done is to establish a border in the dog's life. You have "hedged him in." You have narrowed down his roaming.

This is what child training does. It narrows a child's conduct away from evil and toward godliness; it puts him or her on the right path and in the right direction.

Discipline is used to show the child that when he or she goes beyond the barriers that you have set for him or her, it will be painful. I certainly am not talking about being cruel or abusive, but I am talking about using discipline as a means to teach children about the consequences of going beyond their limited paths. If children do not learn the painful consequences of disobedience and of an unruly life while they are small, then they will find out for sure as they grow older when their consequences will be far greater than a spanking.

Let's look at some verses in Proverbs that talk about parents instructing their children.

- *"My son, hear the instruction of thy father, and forsake not the law of thy mother"* (Proverbs 1:8).

- *"Hear, ye children, the instruction of a father, and attend to know understanding"* (Proverbs 4:1).

- *"He taught me also, and said unto me, Let thine heart retain my words: keep my commandments, and live"* (Proverbs 4:4).

- *"My son, keep thy father's commandment, and forsake not the law of thy mother: Bind them continually upon thine heart, and tie them about thy neck. When thou goest, it shall lead thee; when thou sleepest, it shall keep thee; and when thou awakest, it shall talk with thee. For the commandment is a lamp; and the law is light; and reproofs of instruction are the way of life"* (Proverbs 6:20-23).

From these and other Scriptures in Proverbs, it is evident that God has entrusted parents with the responsibility of instructing their children. It is also plain to see that this instruction is not only based on but also includes the Word of God.

Now let's consider some verses on discipline. Proverbs 19:18 says,

"Chasten thy son while there is hope, and let not thy soul spare for his crying."

Please note the phrase *"while there is hope."* This implies that we can't wait too long to try to train our children. We must start even when they are babies. God knew that parents would be too easy on their children because of their pitiful crying, so He said *"spare not for his crying."* Children soon learn what works to squeeze the heart of mom and dad.

Also we read,

"The rod and reproof give wisdom: but a child left to himself bringeth his mother to shame" (Proverbs 29:15).

There are many today who teach that you should not spank a child. This teaching is enhanced by the reports of so much child abuse. So, in order to stay out of one ditch, they get into another ditch.

My mother and father raised us four children on healthy doses of "hickory tea." They never beat us or abused us, but they did a real good job of teaching us that there is a painful result to disobedience.

In our relationship to our heavenly Father we see this same principle applied.

"For whom the Lord loveth he chasteneth, and scourgeth every son whom he receiveth. If ye endure chastening, God dealeth with you as with sons; for what son is he whom the father chasteneth not? But if ye be without chastisement, whereof all are partakers, then are ye bastards, and not sons." (Hebrews 12:6-8).

Because God loves us, He will chasten us if need be. So we should follow His example and train our children by both instruction and discipline. To put it another way, there are two good tools in training children: a Bible and a little switch or, as some people use, a "spanking spoon."

In Proverbs 29:15, we find the statement,

"a child left to himself bringeth his mother shame."

This is used in the context of discipline. Remember, we have already seen how children are born with a sin nature. They have a natural bent toward sin. If left to themselves, they will surely follow that evil bent.

We see an example of this in Eli and his two sons, Hophni and Phinehas. Eli was the Priest of Shiloh in the days of Samuel's youth. We find his sons described in I Samuel 2:12,

"Now the sons of Eli were sons of Belial, they knew not the Lord."

Then in the last part of verse 25 we read, *"notwithstanding they hearkened not unto the voice of their father."* These two young men were wicked before the Lord and before all Israel. From verse 25, it does appear that Eli tried to teach them better. But when we look at 3:13, we read,

"for I have told him that I will judge his house forever for the iniquity which he knowth; because his sons made themselves vile, and he restrained them not."

God put the blame on both the two sons, and also upon Eli for not restraining them. It appears that Eli did what so many parents do. He may have told them what was right by way of instruction, but he did not back the instructions up with discipline.

Children, even as toddlers, must be taught the association of disobedience with pain. Eli's sons had not been taught that disobedience to God's Word and to their father's instructions would bring severe consequences. For a child the consequences may be a spanking or a privilege taken away, or any other form of discipline. But if that child never learns the lesson of consequences and is left to himself, then as an adult he may make decisions that can have devastating results. All of this is to be instilled in the hearts of children while they are small.

Remember this: a building is no better than its foundation. If the foundation settles, walls will crack, doors and windows will not work properly, and many other problems can occur. So it is with children. Childhood days are the foundational stage of their lives. From those early days, they will build upon what their parents have taught and instilled in them.

Our only hope in preserving the Biblical marriage and the home is to go back to the principles of the Word of God as our guide. We should live these truths and then teach them to our children.

As ministers we should place a great emphasis on Bible exposition on this subject. We should seek to inform and to inspire people to seek the power of God and the help of the

Holy Spirit in their marriages and in their responsibilities of parenting.

Remember, God instituted the home; He as its Creator knows best. To Him be the Glory for a Biblical Marriage and Home!